A RING for the KING

WITHDRAWN

David Lee Morgan Jr.

Shaquille O'Neal and LeBron James dance together during NBA All-Star basketball practice in Las Vegas in February 2007.

TRIUMPH
BOOKS

W9-CJT-883

LeBron James drives past Los Angeles Lakers' Kobe Bryant in February 2007, in Los Angeles.

This book is available in quantity at special discounts for your group or organization.
For further information, contact:
Triumph Books
542 South Dearborn Street
Suite 750
Chicago, Illinois 60605
(312) 939-3330
Fax (312) 663-3557
www.triumphbooks.com

Printed in U.S.A.
ISBN: 978-1-60078-327-2

Design and page production by Mojo Media Inc.
Joe Funk: Editor
Jason Hinman: Creative Director

Photos courtesy of Getty Images unless otherwise noted

AP Images

contents

Introduction

At the time of this book's release, I am 43 years old, and I have been a sportswriter for the *Akron Beacon Journal* for 15 years. In those years, I've had the privilege of covering for this newspaper every sport—at every level—imaginable. Everything from the All-American Soap Box Derby here in Akron at Derby Downs to high school gymnastics, to the Indians in the decisive Game 7 of the World Series, when I watched, from the press box of Pro Player Stadium in Miami, Edgar Renteria dribble a single up the middle in the bottom of the 11th that scored Craig Counsel for a 3–2 Florida Marlins World Series win.

I've had a lot of fun doing my "job," if you want to call what I do a job. I watch sporting events for a living and get paid a decent salary. More than that, though, I love to write and tell stories, so I feel blessed. But I can honestly say that one of the highlights of my career has been covering and watching the development and subsequent meteoric rise of LeBron James.

As author of *LeBron James: The Rise of a Star*, I saw it all. While covering LeBron during all four years of his high school career, I did numerous national radio and television interviews with the likes of John Thompson, Leon Harris of *Headline News*, and Jeremy Schapp of ESPN's *Outside the Lines*, and they were all skeptical. I would always tell reporters that I honestly believed that LeBron was going to be a star. I totally understood their skepticism. But I tried to explain that LeBron was different. He was special. He wasn't like anything anyone had ever seen. So, in my mind, I just stopped trying to tell people how great of a player he was going to be, and I let them *witness* for themselves.

I first met LeBron just before his freshman year at St. Vincent–St. Mary High School. At the time, I was covering high school sports, so I had heard a lot about this kid named LeBron. When his freshman year rolled around, I was assigned to cover LeBron and St. Vincent-St. Mary, along with several other high schools in Akron. But I quickly realized, after watching LeBron and the Irish play, that this was different. It was more than high school basketball. There was something special about LeBron and this group.

They proved that by winning the Division III state championship during LeBron's freshman year, with a 27–0 record. What really amazed me was that LeBron was a starter on a team that played a tough schedule. St. Vincen–St. Mary was a Division III school (there were four divisions), but its schedule was loaded with quality Division I schools from Ohio.

Along with a very skinny, 14-year-old, big-eared, nonathletic looking LeBron, the rest of the team was made up of several of LeBron's close friends, who were

It was clear to nearly every observer that the young high schooler from Akron had a bright future. LeBron James and his whole St. Vincent–St. Mary team had an electricity about them.

the same age and not nearly his size. They all later became known as the "Fab Five."

Maverick Carter, who was a senior and who always told people he and LeBron were cousins (they weren't, but they were so close since they were kids that Maverick should've called him his brother), was the leader and "big brother" of that team.

I was amazed at how St. Vincent–St. Mary rolled through its schedule and finished the year with an unblemished record, despite having a team that relied so heavily on freshmen.

The following year, I continued to cover LeBron and the Irish, and nothing changed. Let me take that back. A lot changed, as far as the reputation that LeBron and his team were starting to build. They were on a mission, and they didn't care who did or did not believe in them; they believed in each other. That confident attitude led St. Vincent–St. Mary to a second straight state championship.

Even looking back now, I remember sharing my thoughts about LeBron to other people, when they would ask how good LeBron *really* was. All I can say is that after his freshman year, I thought, "Man, this kid is going to be a nice Division I college player when it's all said and done."

After his sophomore year, I thought, "Man, this kid could probably start at any Division I major college."

Then after his junior year, I thought, "This kid isn't going to college."

Halfway through LeBron's junior year is when I got the idea to write a book. It was in February 2002 and LeBron had just graced the cover of *Sports Illustrated*.

The day the issue hit the newsstands, St. Vincent–St. Mary held a press conference. It was one of the most surreal atmospheres I have ever been associated with in all of my years covering high school sports.

As I drove up to the school (I lived less than five minutes away), there were television trucks lined all along Maple Street. It was a circus atmosphere. I remember watching grown men with stacks and stacks of *Sports Illustrated* magazines standing at the front door of the school waiting for LeBron to come out so they could get him to sign autographs. It was crazy.

That's when I said to myself, "This is crazy. I have to chronicle this," and decided to write a book.

Not long after the *Sports Illustrated* release, I went to LeBron's mom, Gloria, and told her I wanted to write a book. It wasn't going to be about basketball, though. It was going to be about how a single mother had a son at age 16 and did everything she could to raise that child the right way by herself so that he had a chance in life.

Gloria said she would talk to LeBron about my idea and that she would get back to me. About two weeks later, I approached Gloria and asked her if she and LeBron would be interested, and she replied, "He said 'yeah,' so what you need, baby?"

That was Gloria. Some people could say she was hard, and she was. But if she trusted you and liked you, then you were okay.

LeBron was the same way. In fact, I remember being in Philadelphia just before Christmas in 2002, LeBron's senior year. St. Vincent–St. Mary was playing Philadelphia's Strawberry Mansion, which featured Maureece Rice. There was a sellout crowd of 8,000 people at the famed Palestra, where Rollie Massimino and the Villanova Wildcats gained national fame in the '80s. Philadelphia 76ers guard Allen Iverson was there for the LeBron/Maureece matchup because there was a built-in story line. Rice was closing in on Wilt Chamberlain's city career scoring record, which he eventually broke. But it wasn't broken on this night because LeBron and St. Vincent-St. Mary dominated Strawberry Mansion, the two-time defending

Philadelphia Public League champs, 85–47.

That game was played on my birthday, December 22. But hours before the game, my wife called me and told me a Christmas card came in the mail that day postmarked from Philadelphia.

It baffled me because I was in Philadelphia at the time, and I didn't know anyone from there. So I told my wife to open the card.

When she did, she screamed, "David, oh my God! It's a Christmas card from LeBron."

I said, "What? How could that be? He's in Philadelphia. I'm in Philadelphia. He doesn't even know our address."

My wife said, "David, it's a Christmas card from LeBron. I'm looking right at it."

That blew me away. Not because I got a Christmas card from LeBron, but because he had to take the time to get my address before he left Akron so that he got that card to me, knowing I was going to be in Philadelphia with the team. He knew that because during his senior year, my "beat" was to cover every single game LeBron and St. Vincent–St. Mary played that year, and they played all over the country. Forget the traditional yellow buses. The Irish took charter buses from the school to the Akron-Canton Regional Airport and flew to cities like Philadelphia, Greensboro, N.C., Pittsburgh, and Los Angeles.

That Christmas card meant a lot to me. In fact, not long after that game in Philadelphia, I received a call from Larry Platt, who was the editor of *Philadelphia* magazine and the author of *Only the Strong Survive: The Odyssey of Allen Iverson.*

Larry told me he was writing a feature story in *GQ* magazine about LeBron and wanted to know if he could ask me a few questions. I was delighted to help out in any way. He asked me if there was anything that truly sur-prised me about LeBron. I mentioned to Larry that of all the things that surprised me, it was the Christmas card I received, because to me, it said a lot about the type of heart LeBron had.

Larry's outstanding article, titled "The Fast Education of LeBron James," ran in *GQ* not long after he interviewed me, and I didn't know until a good friend of mine called me.

He said, "David! Man, you're in *GQ*, and LeBron gave you mad props." I didn't know what he was talking about, so he sent me the feature story via email. He told me where to look for my name. And this was the passage:

In his senior year, LeBron was investigated (and ultimately cleared of breaking any rules) by the Ohio High School Athletic Association for receiving a Hummer as a gift and made headlines when he was sus-pended for accepting two throwback jerseys from a Cleveland sporting-goods store. Still, those around him marveled at his perspective, and at a savviness beyond his years. Just days before Christmas 2002, the team traveled to Philadelphia to play a much talked-about game at the famed Palestra against Strawberry Mansion High. When David Lee Morgan, a sports-writer at the Akron Beacon Journal, returned home, there was a holiday card in the mail for him with a Philadelphia postmark. "Dear Mr. Morgan," it read, "Thanks for all your support. LeBron." Asked about the card today, LeBron smiles. "There was a lot of contro-versy going on in the media," he says. "Mr. Morgan was a writer I could trust. I just figured it can't hurt to have a writer like that in your corner."

All I can say is that while covering LeBron, I did my job, I was objective in what I reported, and I was myself, someone who was fair and trustworthy. So I have to admit that it's a good feeling to know that that's what LeBron thought about me. ∎

The Cleveland
SHAQ ATTACK

As far as Shaquille O'Neal was concerned, the Cleveland Cavaliers' quest for an NBA world championship started the day the "Big Fella" arrived in Cleveland, specifically, at the Cavaliers' training facility in Independence, Ohio. The facility is about 20 minutes from The Q, the Cavaliers' home arena in downtown Cleveland, and about the same distance from the home of "the King," LeBron James.

Shaq, sporting a grin as big and wide as his 7-foot-1, 325-pound frame, walked into the gym and handed out high fives to a long reception line of area kids who were thrilled to get the chance to touch a hand almost 10 times the size of their own little hands. Shaq seemed to love it just as much as the children. His press conference seemed to be that of a new sheriff coming into town to put the townsfolk at ease. Shaq was coming to the rescue, and the poor, suffering fans in Cleveland needed all the help they could get.

Shaq became a member of the Cavaliers on June 25, 2009, when the organization made a bold move in announcing it had acquired the 15-time NBA All-Star who had won four NBA World Championships—three in a row with the Los Angeles Lakers from 2000 to 2002 and one with the Miami Heat in 2006. In all, he has reached the NBA Finals six times.

Now, LeBron and the Cavaliers were getting that legitimate, big-name, proven center, that and a player with extensive NBA championship experience that the King desperately needed.

Was Shaq going to be the final missing piece to the puzzle that would finally get LeBron his ring?

It was obvious that Shaq was excited to be in Cleveland, even when you consider the fact that he had only played in warm-weather cities: Los Angeles, Miami, and Phoenix.

"I'd like to thank the owner, Dan Gilbert, and the great Danny Ferry for bringing me here because

A 15-time All-Star and a four-time NBA champion, Shaq brings wisdom and experience along with his body-bruising style of play to the Cavaliers. He may be the final piece to Cleveland's championship puzzle.

NBAE / Getty Images

we all know Danny was a great player. The other day when I got the call from Danny Ferry, I kept thinking, 'Danny Ferry, Danny Ferry.' So I had to check my computer to see who Danny Ferry was, and this is what came up on the Internet."

At that moment, Shaq showed he was going to fit right in with LeBron when it came to having a sense of humor and being lighthearted in somewhat serious situations. Shaq unrolled a picture of himself and Ferry on the basketball court as professionals. The photo showed Shaq seemingly hugging Ferry on the court while Ferry was bending over trying to gain possession of the basketball.

In a different setting, the photo could have been used for blackmail purposes, because it was an awkward pose. Everyone inside the practice facility attending the press conference burst out in laughter when Shaq revealed the picture. And that's how Shaq arrived onto the Cleveland scene.

Shaq proved that having the opportunity to play with a future Hall of Famer like LeBron James, even if it was in a mid-market city like Cleveland, was enough for him. He was going to have fun in Cleveland playing with LeBron, and he was going to do everything in his power to win yet another world championship. He didn't care that the spotlight *wasn't* going to be on him.

All that mattered was that Shaq wanted to win a *Ring for the King*.

"Now, I'm playing with one of the greatest players

(above) Smiling with Mike Brown and Danny Ferry at his introduction as a Cleveland Cavalier, Shaq had plenty of praise for the organization and the men that brought him to Cleveland. (opposite) There is one goal in mind for the beaming Shaq, to wear his jersey with pride and bring a championship to Cleveland and win a *Ring for the King*.

so that should make the game very, very easy for me," Shaq said. "I put LeBron up there with Tim Duncan as the most intelligent players in the game today."

That was a very insightful comment for Shaq to make, until he revealed the source of such a wise and thoughtful observation. "I stole that from (Cavaliers) Coach (Mike) Brown. Coach Brown told me that last night." The crowd erupted in laughter as if Shaq was in the middle of a 30-minute set at the world-famous Improv Comedy Club. "When he said that, I had to quickly agree."

What some critics didn't agree with was the fact that Shaq, at the ripe old NBA age of 37, with all of the ailments and injuries and wear and tear, was the answer and the missing piece of the puzzle for the Cavaliers.

Critics hailed the signing as yet another bad move in Cleveland sports history. They said O'Neal would only slow LeBron and the Cavaliers down. They said Shaq slowed down the Suns' high-octane offense in his 1½ years with Phoenix. Shaq did a respectable job with the Suns, averaging 15 points and nine rebounds for the team, but there were times, and they were often, critics said, when Shaq looked his age.

At the same time, critics said the same thing about Cavaliers veteran center Zydrunas Ilgauskas, who was clearly overmatched against the Orlando Magic's youthful center Dwight Howard, who was nearly unstoppable against Ilagauskas and the Cavaliers in the 2009 Eastern Conference Finals series, which Orlando won four games to two.

During that series, Howard scored a series-high 44 points in the sixth and deciding game. That's why Ferry made the deal to acquire O'Neal—because, more than anything, Shaq's size would give Cleveland a little more muscle inside.

But as far as Shaq was concerned, his age and health weren't going to be an issue. "I got a lot left," he said. "I've been (in the league) 17 years, but I think I missed three years worth of injuries so if you do the math, I still have three years left."

And Shaq commented that he can still run the floor when needed. "I'm pretty much able to play any style. I realize that big guys most of the time are going to get rebounds so I'm going to be getting the rebounds and slinging it to (Cavaliers point guard) Mo (Williams) or LeBron and let them do what they do."

Shaq must've also realized he went too long without delivering a punch line, which he quickly produced like a seasoned comedian always wanting his audience to anticipate the next joke.

"As long as I get a couple drop-offs...I'm not here to demand 40 or 50 (shots a game)...I would just like 30," Shaq said, as the crowd burst into laughter once again. All that Shaq needed to finish off the joke was a guy in a polyester suit on a drum set in the background producing a snare drum–rim shot–cymbal

By his way of thinking, the big man still has three years left in his gas tank. He can play any style of basketball, and his work inside will bring a dominant presence to the post that the Cavaliers have sorely missed.

combination symbolizing an exquisitely delivered punch line.

Then Shaq continued, "I'm just coming to do my part and help a damn good team."

One thing that Shaq had always been serious and passionate about, other than basketball, was law enforcement. While he was playing for the Miami Heat and the Phoenix Suns, he was deputized and received honorary badges in Arizona and Florida.

During the press conference at the Cavaliers' practice facility, Shaq was asked by a reporter, "Will there be any involvement from you towards our law enforcement agencies here in Northeast Ohio?"

Shaq's response?

"I'm actually undercover, so I really can't answer that." (Cue drummer with the rim shot and cymbals.)

And for a moment, Shaq spoke in a serious tone. "Everybody knows I'm very interested in law enforcement, and when the time comes, we'll have that conversation," said Shaq. "But now, my motto is very simple: win a ring for the King."

Instead of laughter, the crowd erupted with applause.

To Shaq, getting a ring means establishing team unity and having everyone on the same page. Although he won three championships in Los Angeles, it was well-chronicled how he had a tumultuous relationship with Kobe Bryant. "I'm not going to do it by myself, and LeBron is not going to try to

do it by himself," Shaq said. "It's going to take a team, city, and organizational effort to get it done, but we definitely have all the pieces here so there will be no excuses. The expectations are high, and we want them to be high. That's what thrives and motivates us, and we'll be ready."

The relationship between LeBron and Shaq goes back to LeBron's high school days, when the Heat was in Cleveland to play the Cavaliers. LeBron was playing in a game for St. Vincent–St. Mary in

(above) O'Neal has maintained an interest in law enforcement throughout his NBA career and has been deputized in both Florida and Arizona. He joked about his interest in law enforcement in Ohio, but reiterated that his emphasis is on winning a crown in Cleveland. (opposite) Shaq and Kobe may have had a tumultuous relationship in Los Angeles, but the combination was lethal to the rest of the NBA. The pair won three straight NBA titles together.

nearby Canton, the home of the Pro Football Hall of Fame. Shaq decided to take in LeBron's game the day before he and the Heat were scheduled to play in Cleveland, about 40 miles north of Canton.

Shaq was impressed with LeBron back then. "I knew he was a special player then because when I went to see him in high school, I saw a freakish athlete that was bigger and stronger than everybody," Shaq said. "For example, like me, when I was in high school and playing against smaller guys like (joke alert) Danny Ferry (laughter), I was just trying to score, score, score. But LeBron was getting all of his teammates involved, guys that (might not ever) play on the college level and would never make it to the NBA level. He was drawing defenders and kicking the ball out to his guys.

"I was telling (former NBA star) Ron Harper then that this kid was special and that he was very humble," O'Neal added. "He's made a name for himself and he's done it the right and respectful way, so for me and the last few years of my career, I'm honored to play with the great LeBron James."

Then, Shaq was asked what it would be like in June 2010, if it became a Cavaliers vs. Lakers, LeBron vs. Kobe NBA finals.

There was no punch line from Shaq. It was all business. All serious.

"You know what, from my experience, when I don't talk about it, it usually gets done," Shaq said.

"So my motto is simple, win a ring for the King. Take care of business and see what happens. I'm not going to waste time this year talking about possible matchups. We still got October, November...we still have to get it done."

Then came the humor.

"I'll probably just talk about it once or twice, and I don't mention it again," Shaq said. "But to answer your question, that would be a hell of a matchup," Shaq added, with his trademark smile.

The crowd burst into laughter once again.

Officially, Cleveland got O'Neal in exchange for forward/center Ben Wallace, guard/forward Sasha Pavlovic, Cleveland's second-round pick in the 2010 NBA Draft (top 40 protected), and cash considerations. "It is a really unique and rare opportunity to bring in a player of Shaq's caliber," said Ferry, who seemed to have a respectable and admirable relationship with Shaq as a former opponent during their league years and now as a member of the same team. "We are excited to see how his presence, experience, and play positively impacts our team."

In the same breath, Ferry commended the players who were heading out to Phoenix for their service in Cleveland. Pavlovic was solid with the Cavaliers and showed loads of potential. But he was inconsistent offensively and was a liability on defense.

Pavlovic played in 66 games (12 starts) during the 2008–09 season with the Cavaliers and aver-

The Big Aristotle has always had an admiration for LeBron, dating back to the King's prep days. He's looking forward to bringing a title to Cleveland—even if that means going through Kobe and the Lakers.

LeBron and Shaq have had the chance to bond at NBA All-Star festivities in the past, and the two are certain they will have chemistry on the floor when it is crunch time.

aged 4.6 points and 1.9 rebounds in 15.9 minutes per game. In 302 games with Cleveland, he averaged 6.1 points on .417 shooting, including shooting .374 from three-point range, and 1.9 rebounds in 18.0 minutes per game.

Wallace, acquired by the Cavaliers on February 21, 2008, from Chicago, played in 78 games with Cleveland and posted averages of 3.3 points, 6.7 rebounds, and 1.4 blocks in 24.2 minutes per game. A four-time Defensive Player of the Year and All-Star selection, Wallace had career averages of 6.2 points on .472 shooting, 10.3 rebounds, and 2.2 blocks in 30.9 minutes per game.

Wallace was a fan favorite and was a hard worker with the Cavaliers. He was slowed toward the end of the season with injuries. Ferry and the organization felt it was time to head in another direction with Pavlovic and Wallace.

"We truly appreciate all that Ben and Sasha gave to this team and community in their time here," Ferry said. "They were good teammates, and we wish them nothing but success."

The file on O'Neal:

• He is a 15-time NBA All-Star and four-time NBA champion. With Phoenix during the 2008–2009 season, he played in 75 games, which were all starts, and averaged 17.8 points, 8.4 rebounds, 1.7 assists, and 1.4 blocks in 30.1 minutes per game. His 75 games played were the most in a season since the 1999–2000 campaign, and his scoring average of 17.8 was his highest since the 2005–06 season. More impressive was that he shot a career- and NBA-best 61 percent from the field.

• He was named an All-Star during the 2008–2009 season for the 15th time, the second-most in NBA history, and shared All-Star Game MVP honors with the Los Angeles Lakers' Kobe Bryant, following a 17-point, five-rebound, three-assist outing in the West's 146–119 victory. Following the season, he was named to the All-NBA Third Team, marking the 14th time he has earned All-NBA honors.

• He finished the season as the fifth-leading scorer in NBA history with 27,619 career points and joined Kareem Abdul-Jabbar as the only players in NBA history with at least 27,000 points, 12,000 rebounds, and 2,500 blocks in their careers. In leading the NBA in field-goal percentage for the 10th time, he set an NBA record, breaking the mark he previously shared with Wilt Chamberlain. He owned the second-highest field-goal percentage in NBA history, with a career mark of .582. He ranked seventh on the NBA's all-time blocked-shots list with 2,628 and 15th in rebounds, with 12,566 total boards.

As shown by his All-Star co-MVP award in 2009, O'Neal is much more than an aging big name. He's still a force to be reckoned with in the NBA, and the move to Cleveland will help complete his career rejuvenation.

• O'Neal is also the NBA's active leader in points (27,619), offensive rebounds (4,068), total rebounds (12,566), free throw attempts (10,895), and field-goal percentage (.582).

Shaq's signing was big news in Cleveland and throughout the NBA but not as big as the speculation that surrounded LeBron and his future in Cleveland. In fact, the summer of 2010 is expected to be one of the more notable summers in NBA history when it comes to high-profile names such as Dwayne Wade, Chris Bosh, Amare Stoudemire, Steve Nash, Dirk Nowitzki, and Michael Redd, who are expected to test the market.

LeBron's contract also was to expire at the end of the 2010 season, and according to the NBA collective bargaining agreement, the Cavaliers would be permitted to exceed the salary cap to sign him for six years.

LeBron, however, never really wanted to get into particulars about his contract as it related to him staying in Cleveland and in his native Northeast Ohio or leaving for a larger market, such as New York, which always seemed to be the talk. Ferry, meanwhile, always felt confident LeBron would remain a Cavalier.

"For LeBron it is about more than just dollars,"

(above) The owner of one of the highest field-goal percentages in NBA history, Shaq is statistically one of the most prolific players to ever play the game. He dominates the game above the rim, in the paint, and with his considerable bulk. (opposite) Although the 2009 offseason has been an exciting one for the Cavaliers and their fans, all eyes are on the 2010 free agency season. Several big names, including LeBron James, are scheduled to hit the market.

Ferry said. "As an organization we have committed to building a championship-level team for years to come. There's a lot of attention and speculation about his future. LeBron has conveyed that he enjoys playing and living in Northeast Ohio."

LeBron told Tom Withers of the Associated Press: "Every day it seems like (the media) has me going someplace else. I'm very happy here; I have said that over and over."

LeBron signed a three-year contract in 2006 and has an option for the 2010–11 season. He has until June 30, 2010, to extend the contract or pick up the option year. The Cavaliers offered James a contract extension on July 18, 2009, but LeBron told Withers in August 2009 that he would be unlikely to accept a contract extension from the Cavaliers until after the 2009–2010 season. "I signed a contract in 2006 with an option, and it would make no sense for me to sign that contract if I didn't keep my options open," he said. "I'll let you fill in the blanks."

In the meantime, LeBron wanted to focus on the 2010 season and playing with Shaq. "To get the opportunity to play with one of the greatest basketball players to ever play the game, that's the fun part for me," LeBron told the Associated Press. "I'm humbled by that."

If you thought LeBron was outstanding in 2009, when he averaged 28.4 points, 7.6 rebounds, and 7.2 assists during the regular season and 35.3 points, 9.1 rebounds, and 7.3 assists in the playoffs and won the league MVP award, LeBron said he expected to be an even bigger offensive threat in 2010 with the addition of Shaq.

"I can use some of my athleticism when a double-team comes and slash to the rim," he told reporters. "Shaq's a very good passer, so he'll just throw it at the rim, and I'll go get it. Instead of dribbling the ball up where guys can pressure me, I can catch the ball out of a double-team from Shaq, become a shooter, or drive."

As a guest speaker at the National Association of Black Journalists convention, LeBron talked about having Shaq in Cleveland.

"I've never had a low-post presence since I've been in the league," LeBron said. "I love it. I can defer to a teammate. If Shaq is going *I'm OK,* and if it's one of those nights when he isn't feeling it, I can take over … I know one thing that's going to happen; you can't check Shaq one-on-one. I can use some of my athleticism when a double-team comes and slash to the rim. If I catch the ball in the spot-up [position], I can either drive it or pass it. You're at my mercy."

As much fun as Shaq was having just *talking* about his future in Cleveland with LeBron, he was having just as much fun with his many ventures off the court, such as his television show *Shaq Vs.*, which premiered on ABC in the summer of

LeBron has said it time and again—the King is happy to extend his monarchy in Cleveland—but wants to wait until the end of the 2009–2010 season to explore all of his options.

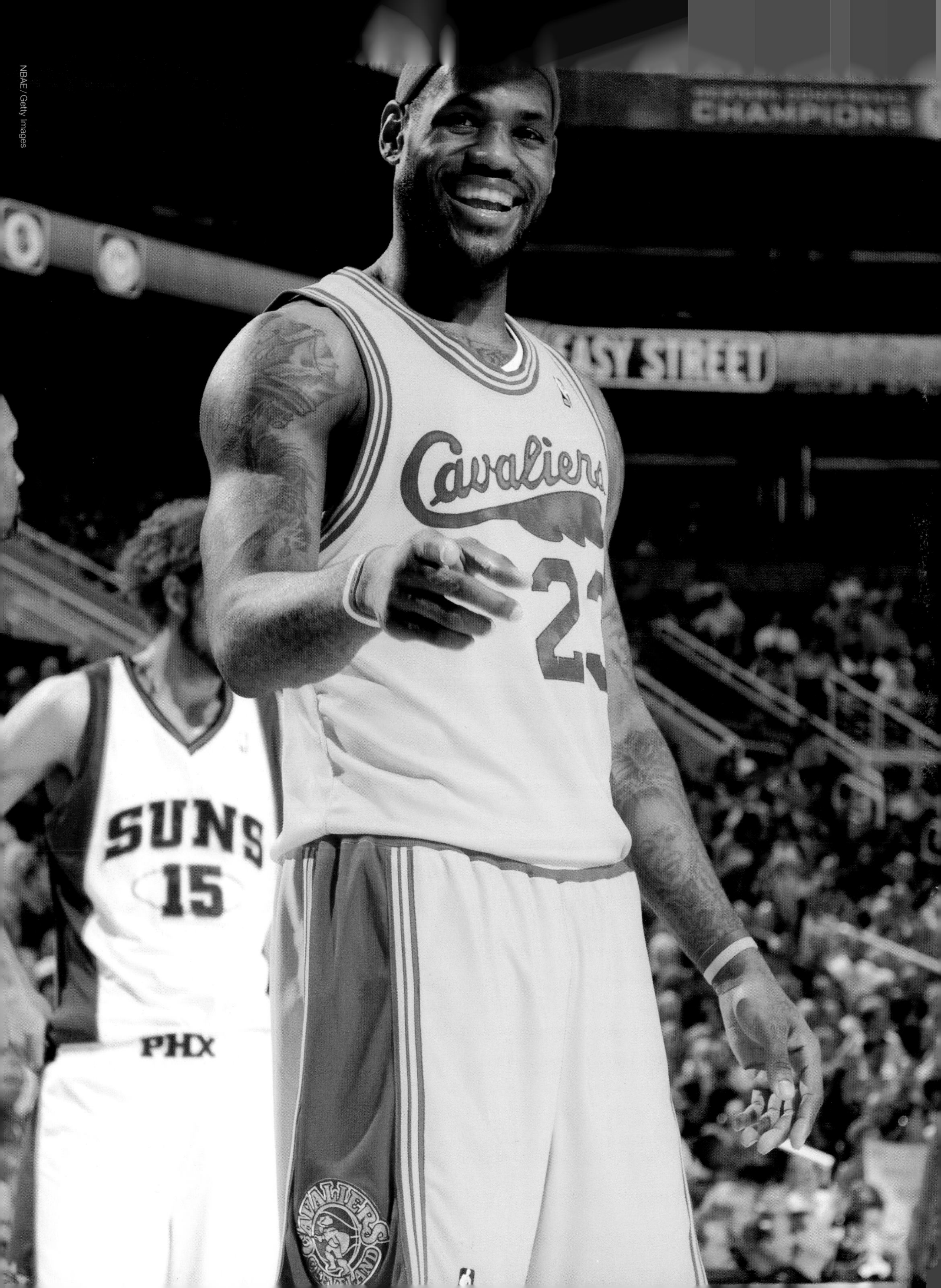

NBAE / Getty Images

2009. The show consists of Shaq taking on other top-level professional athletes such as Olympic and World Champion Michael Phelps in the swimming pool; Pittsburgh Steelers and Super Bowl champion quarterback Ben Roethlisberger on the football field; U.S. Open, Australian Open, and Wimbledon champion Serena Williams in tennis; former boxing champ Oscar De La Hoya in boxing; two-time National League MVP and St. Louis Cardinals first baseman Albert Pujols in baseball; and Olympic gold medalists Kerri Walsh and Misty May-Treanor in beach volleyball.

A die-hard Cavaliers fan wrote an open letter to me about Cleveland's chances of winning a championship with Shaq, and it seems to reflect the consensus among most Northeast Ohio Fans. He wrote:

Early on in the playoff series with the Orlando Magic, it was obvious to me and most knowledgeable basketball fans that the Cavaliers were going to come up short in their quest for an NBA championship. They didn't have an answer for the stellar outside shooting of the much taller Orlando guards as well as the dominating play of the young, powerful, talented center Dwight Howard, in the painted area.

The off-season trades by the Cavalier management were very interesting, to say the least. I have

(above) While he's all business on the court, Shaq is determined to enjoy his time off it. His ventures include his reality series *Shaq Vs.,* featuring the big man taking on athletes in their own sports. Here, he poses with boxing legend Oscar De La Hoya. (opposite) 2009 was the "Summer of Shaq," as his show took him all over the country. This press conference promoted his challenge against beach volleyball superstars Keri Walsh and Misty May-Treanor.

to give the front office props for an excellent effort to surround LeBron James with enough talent to take this team to the NBA championship, with the goal of winning it all, not just getting into the big game. The biggest acquisition, of course, was the addition of perennial All-Star Shaquille O'Neal, who seemed to be reborn last season. It's almost ironic that O'Neal will now be playing in most likely his final season in the NBA with a kid named LeBron, who he had enough of an interest in to stop by and watch one of his high school basketball games.

Shaq looked very good last season, and to me it seems like he really wants to go out on top. It adds to the intrigue of two mega-superstars playing together on an already very polished Cavaliers basketball team.

Shaq stated publicly that he will be in top shape when camp breaks, and he is very serious about putting another championship ring on his finger and helping his friend LeBron James to get his first. The downside with Shaq is his horrendous free throw shooting. Just like former Cavalier Ben Wallace, Shaq is a liability in the fourth quarter when shooting free throws. Teams will employ the "Hackey Shaq" strategy and purposely foul him, betting that he will miss one or both tries most of the time. But Shaq has more to offer than Ben Wallace and will bring a dominating force inside unlike the Cavs have ever seen before. The Cavs could also get creative

and play Zydrunas Ilgauskas and O'Neal together to give them an inside/outside threat from two All-Star seven footers.

It would have been especially nice if the Cavs had picked up free agent forward Rasheed Wallace to combat Orlando's three-point threat, but they didn't get him. They did, however, pick up Leon Powe from the Boston Celtics. This pick-up will also strengthen the team. In my opinion, the Cavs front office made a very good effort to bring enough talent to the Cavaliers to get them over the hump and to the next level. My gut feeling is that the Cavaliers will definitely be a better basketball team. But as far as winning it all, I have mixed emotions. I honestly believe that they have enough weapons to win it all, but I also believe that they could possibly come up short again to the Lakers or Orlando. This season will be exciting, but as far as winning the ring...only time will tell.

Thanks for your time,
—Mike Ede

Some fans may worry about weaknesses in the Cavs' game—including Shaq's free-throw shooting—but part of the excitement is waiting to see what will happen.

The time is right for the core of
the Cavs to jell and win an NBA title.
The veteran leadership is there, the
superstar has come into his own, and
the team is hungrier than ever after
deep runs in the playoffs.

Making the Right Moves for
A CHAMPIONSHIP

Despite losing in the 2009 Eastern Conference Finals to Orlando (four games to two), the Cavaliers were quick to look to the 2010 season as another year of contention for an NBA championship. The front office made solid moves to acquire even better talent than the previous season by signing Shaquille O'Neal and forwards Anthony Parker and Jamario Moon.

Will that be enough?

What will it take for the Cavaliers to win it all?

SHAQ, RATTLE, AND ROLL

If Shaq says he still has a few years in him, Cavaliers fans need to see it. Last season, Shaq had the best field-goal percentage in his career, shooting 61 percent from the field. You can dissect that many different ways to support or discredit that stat, but the truth is that once Shaq gets within two feet of the basket, he's hard to stop because of his size and strength. It will be interesting to see how many minutes Shaq plays per game, with the

"Godfather" of the Cavaliers' organization, Zydrunas Ilgauskas, still producing (at least offensively). Obviously, the two won't be on the court at the same time, but the bottom line is that the play that comes out of the center position will be the biggest reason the Cavaliers make it to the finals, if they do at all.

S.F. (STAGE FRIGHT) SYNDROME

The Cavaliers have to shake that "Stage Fright Syndrome" they seemed to have against the Magic in the Eastern Conference Finals. Granted, Orlando center Dwight Howard was more athletic and talented than Zydrunas Ilgauskas and was nearly unstoppable during that series. But Howard wasn't invincible, as the Lakers showed during the NBA Finals. Outside of LeBron, Cleveland showed no consistency on offense or defense against Orlando. The Cavaliers cruised through the first two rounds of the playoffs against Detroit and Atlanta, but when it was crunch time, they wilted. The Cavaliers

Zydrunas Ilgauskas tried his best against Dwight Howard in the playoffs, but Orlando was able to exploit soft spots in the Cavs' game to knock Cleveland out of the running. After coasting through the first two rounds of the playoffs, inconsistency and the Magic smacked them down.

The Orlando series was a tough challenge, a wake-up
call and a growing experience for the Cavaliers.
Looking for a trump card in 2009–2010, the team
may have found it in Shaquille O'Neal.

seemed to have the right chemistry all season. The team was loose and confident—maybe too loose—after sweeping Detroit and Atlanta. There were times during the Detroit series when players were laughing and joking on the bench. But the Cavaliers had no answer for Howard and the Magic, and critics were quick to point out once again that the Cavaliers lacked that killer instinct and couldn't win the big game. Maybe Shaq will bring that much-needed "crunch time" swagger the Cavaliers need to get over the top.

QUICK CHEMISTRY

One of the things that made the Cavaliers strong last year was the team chemistry. The team was cohesive, and when it was hit with injuries to starters, other players stepped up, and the squad didn't miss a beat. The Cavaliers acquired Delonte West, Wally Szczerbiak, Ben Wallace, and Joe Smith during the 2007–2008 season. It took them time to develop chemistry, but as veteran players they made the transition seamless. It was obvious this team cared about each other and enjoyed playing the game together. Now that the Cavaliers acquired All-Star center Shaquille O'Neal and forwards Anthony Parker and Jamario Moon, those players must make the transition smooth and help develop that team chemistry as soon as possible.

DEPTH PERCEPTION

There was a point during the 2008–2009 season when it was okay if LeBron left the court for an

(above) One of the hallmarks of the Cavaliers is their team chemistry. Loose on the bench, playful, and fun, the team truly enjoys playing together. They must now take the next step and turn that chemistry into big-game mental toughness. (opposite) In addition to Shaq, free-agent signees Anthony Parker and Jamario Moon (pictured) will have to mesh with their new teammates to make the Cavs better. Other additions have fit in LeBron's supporting cast, so the new trio should click in just fine.

extended period of time to catch a breather. But during the Orlando series, LeBron was the only reason the scores were as close as they were. For the 2009–2010 season, the Cavaliers need to establish that they can play with anyone, regardless of whether LeBron is on the court. The truth is that LeBron is such a force on the court that when he's off the court, opposing teams have a different attitude toward the Cavaliers. More than one player (dozens and dozens) has stated that, just not on the record. The Cavaliers' play can't drop drastically when LeBron is off the court.

Are Cavaliers fans excited for the start of the season, even after a heartbreaking loss to Orlando in the conference finals?

Absolutely. As long as Cleveland has LeBron and Shaq, anything is possible, right?

That feeling of disappointment for Cavaliers' fans after the Orlando series started to fade somewhat on June 25, 2009, when the Cavaliers signed Shaq. Then, Ferry started making moves, one after another. Two weeks after signing Shaq, the Cavaliers locked up one of its fan favorites in 6-foot-11 forward Anderson Varejao to a multiyear contract. More than anything, Ferry, LeBron, and Cavaliers fans love Varejao's high-energy level of play. He wasn't going to score a lot of points, but he did all the little things for the Cavaliers. He had the intangibles. If you needed him to dive into the stands or on the ground for a loose ball, he did it. If you needed him to dominate the offensive boards and keep a possession alive, he did. And if you needed him to take a charge at a crucial time in a game, he was one of the best—so good that opponents often complained to the officials that he was doing more flopping and acting than anything else. The truth was that Varejao was outstanding at anticipating when an offensive player was going to make a strong move to the basket, and he had a knack for stepping in the lane at the right moment to take a charge.

How effective was he at this practice? He was second in the NBA in drawing offensive charges, with 52. Varejao wasn't known for his scoring, but in 2009, he posted career-bests in points per game (8.6), field-goal percentage (.536), double doubles (9), minutes per game (28.5), and starts (42) in 81 games played and averaged 7.2 rebounds and 1.0 assist per game. But in the 42 games he started, he increased his averages to 9.9 points and 7.7 rebounds per game.

"We are very happy to announce that we have agreed to a multiyear contract with Anderson," Ferry said about the move. "From the start of free agency, Anderson made it clear he wanted to be a part of our future and that he loved being in Cleveland. For us, we have been one of the better teams in the NBA the past four years. Andy has

There are only a handful of players in the NBA capable of drawing a charge like Anderson Varejao. His success on the defensive end of the floor translated to the offensive side as well—he posted career numbers in 2008–2009.

NBAE /Getty Images

played an important role with our team during that time, and continuity is important to us. He brings many valued contributions to our team on and off the court and plays with relentless passion and energy every play. He is an elite defender, and we want to continue building our strong defensive identity."

Against Chicago on January 2, 2009, he posted career highs in scoring (26), field goals made (9) and attempted (14), and free throws made (8) and attempted (13). He tied his career best in rebounding with 14 at Toronto on February 18 and went a perfect 8–8 from the field on his way to an 18-point, 12-rebound double double at Sacramento on March 13th. He scored in double figures on 30 occasions (the Cavaliers were 25–5 in those games) and

topped the 10-rebound mark 15 times on the season.

Varejao also was selected as a member of *USA Today*'s 2009 All-Rambis Team. Just what is the All-Rambis Team? It's a team named after former NBA forward Kurt Rambis, who played from 1981 to 1995. Rambis averaged 5.2 points, 5.6 rebounds, and 18.5 minutes per game in his career and was known for his years with the Lakers during the Magic Johnson, Kareem Abdul-Jabbar "Showtime" days. Rambis was the ultimate role player. He had long hair, wore thick black-rimmed glasses, and although he just didn't look like the L.A. type on the court, he was effective in playing his role. Rambis was what Dennis Rodman was back in his successful championship days with the Detroit Pistons, only Rambis

(above) The Chicago Bulls had their hands full with Varejao on January 2, 2009. The Cavs' number one role player stepped into the limelight for the night, pouring in a career-high 26 points. (opposite) Though it may not always be pretty, Varejao has carved out a distinct niche for himself. He is one of the best role players in the NBA, a job recognized by *USA Today* when it selected him for its All-Rambis team—a reference to former blue-collar member of the Lakers during the Showtime era, and newly minted coach of the Minnesota Timberwolves, Kurt Rambis.

didn't wear makeup, dress up in a wedding gown for a publicity stunt, dye his hair a multitude of colors, or have numerous piercings and tattoos.

So Rambis, who went on to be a successful assistant with the Lakers under head coach Phil Jackson, explained in *USA Today* what it took to make his team.

"The guy can't be afraid to throw his body around," Rambis said. "He must be completely unselfish about his game and give of himself for the benefit of his team. He's going to have to do a lot of things that won't show up in the box score, but he's going to be the guy on his team that his teammates appreciate more than anybody else.

"Diving on the floor, setting picks, getting rebounds, taking the tough defensive assignments," Rambis said. "But he also must be able to do enough offensively to keep his man occupied, so he can't just go out and double-team somebody."

Just a few days after signing Varejao to a multi-year deal, the Cavaliers signed another member of the 2009 *USA Today* All-Rambis Team in 6-foot-6, 210-pound guard/forward Anthony Parker, 34, who played in 80 games (71 starts) in 2009 for the Toronto Raptors and averaged 10.7 points, 4.0 rebounds, and career highs of 3.4 assists and 1.3 steals in 33.0 minutes per game. He tied for 10th in the NBA with a 0.88 steal-per-turnover ratio and recorded a career-high 100 steals. He was one of just 11 players in the NBA to total at least 750 points, 250 rebounds, 250 assists, and 100 steals during the 2008–09 season.

Rambis said of Parker: "He takes a lot of pride in doing the little things, guarding the other team's best player, diving for loose balls. You have to do your best every night, no matter what."

Parker also showed he could do a little scoring, and that should help the Cavaliers, considering the backcourt scoring against Orlando was inconsistent.

In a regular-season game against Orlando on January 4, Parker scored a season-high 26 points on 13-of-16 shooting from the field.

"Anthony will be a solid addition to our roster. He is a very good, intelligent all-around basketball player," Ferry said. "Our coaching staff will especially appreciate the good shooting and solid defense that Anthony brings to our team."

In six years in the NBA, Parker averaged 10.1 points and 3.4 rebounds a game. But before he entered the NBA, he played five seasons with Maccabi Tel Aviv and one season with Virtus Roma. He had championship experience while playing in Europe, and although it wasn't the NBA, playing in a setting like that helped Parker understand what postseason play is all about. The Cavaliers are hoping he can bring that mentality to the team.

Parker won five Israeli Premier League championships, five Israeli Cups, and three Euroleague

Versatile and a consistent scoring threat, Anthony Parker commands the attention of every opponent and is sure to be a spark plug for the Cavaliers.

titles and was named Euroleague MVP and first-team All-Euroleague in 2005. He averaged 12.4 points, 4.8 rebounds, 3.4 assists, and 1.6 steals in 148 career Israeli Premier League games and averaged 16.3 points, 5.8 rebounds, 3.2 assists, and 1.6 steals in 90 Euroleague games.

The Cavaliers' thought heading into the 2010 season was to either start Parker or have him come off the bench behind Delonte West. Regardless of where Parker fits in, he is a good fit for the Cavaliers in their attempt at an NBA championship run.

The next move Ferry made was signing restricted free agent forward Jamario Moon on July 24. The Cavaliers signed Moon to a contract offer sheet a week

before, and the Miami Heat declined to match their offer. "Jamario is going to bring versatility and a high level of athleticism to our team," Ferry said about this acquisition. "He should be a very good fit to our current roster. We are very happy to have him with us."

Moon, a 6-8 forward, played in 80 games (60 starts) for Toronto and the Heat the previous season, where he averaged 7.2 points, 4.6 rebounds, 1.2 assists, and 1.1 steals in 25.8 minutes per game. What Ferry liked about Moon was the fact that he is very efficient on offense. He isn't a big scorer, but he takes care of the ball when it is in his hands, and when he is on defense, he has a knack for coming up with the ball. He led the NBA in steals-to-turnovers

(above) Wherever he ends up playing in the Cleveland rotation, Parker will excel. His do-whatever-it-takes attitude will help him fit in with his new teammates and make him a fan fave. (opposite) When Jamario Moon puts up a shot, it's usually a good one. He doesn't set the world on fire offensively, but he takes care of the ball and scores timely baskets.

ratio (2.0) during the 2008–09 season.

The last move Ferry made before the Cavaliers headed into preseason camp for the 2010 season was signing 25-year-old free agent forward Leon Powe on August 12. Powe averaged 7.7 points on .524 shooting and a career-best 4.9 rebounds in 17.5 minutes per game during the previous season with Boston. But in his seven starts, he averaged 14.3 points on .576 shooting, 8.1 rebounds, and 1.4 blocks in 25.9 minutes per game. He recorded career highs in scoring (30), blocks (5), and assists (3) and added 11 rebounds in 41 minutes versus Memphis on March 13.

The only concern the Cavaliers had was the fact that Powe suffered a torn ACL and meniscus in his left knee in Game 2 of the first round of the 2009 playoffs against the Chicago Bulls. He ended up missing the rest of the playoffs.

"Leon is a high-quality player and person. His tough, gritty play has already contributed in big playoff games during his young career," Ferry said. "As he continues to work at rehabilitating his injury, we would look to hopefully see him return towards the end of the season."

And Cavs fans can feel optimistic about the return of 6-foot-9, 242-pound second-year forward J.J. Hickson. The Cavs' 2008 first-round selection (19th pick overall) came off the bench and averaged 4.0 points and 2.7 rebounds per game in his rookie season. Ferry has been high on the youngsters potential to be a solid forward in the league as he matures and develops, mentallly and physically.

On November 26, 2008, Hickson scored a career-high 14 points along with six rebounds and four blocked shots against the Oklahoma City Thunder. But a back injury in April sidelined him for the season and he missed the last 20 games.

Meanwhile, if there is a watershed moment in Cleveland Cavaliers' history, is this it?

Is it all or nothing this year? If the Cavaliers don't win it all, is LeBron *LeGone*? It should be an interesting story.

The history between LeBron and the Cavaliers dates back to LeBron's senior year at St. Vincent–St. Mary High School. Local Cavaliers fans joked that LeBron's team could've given the Cavaliers a run for their money that season. On that 2002–2003 Cavaliers team were Milt Palacio, Smush Parker, Tierre Brown, Jumaine Jones, Michael Stewart, Chris Mihm, Dajuan Wagner, and Bimbo Coles, none of whom were necessarily household names. That Cavaliers team went 17–65 and played in front of sparse crowds, while LeBron and the Irish were playing in front of sellout crowds in college arenas.

However, the Cavaliers' dismal record helped them get the No. 1 pick in 2003 in hometown hero LeBron James, and the rest is draft history for the Cavaliers. The only player on that 2002–2003 Cavaliers roster who was still with the team heading into the 2009–2010 season was Ilgauskas.

Cavs management thought that the LeBron-Ilgauskas tandem would form the nucleus as it rebuilt the franchise. As LeBron has flourished, however, it's become apparent that he needs a more versatile supporting cast.

The organization felt at that time that "Z" and LeBron would be the nucleus, the players of the future, and management would build from there. Since LeBron's rookie season in 2003, it was obvious that he was going to need more help than just Z if the Cavaliers were going to contend for an NBA championship. When successful businessman Dan Gilbert bought the team from Gordon Gund in 2005, Gilbert's main goal was to do whatever it took to bring in the pieces that would help LeBron and the Cavaliers win a world championship.

When Gilbert, chairman and founder of the nation's largest online home lender, Quicken Loans, and Michigan-based home mortgage company Rock Financial, bought the team, he hired former Duke All-American and Cavaliers player Danny Ferry as the general manager and Mike Brown, a well-respected assistant coach with the Indiana Pacers at the time, as the head coach.

Gilbert, Ferry, Brown, and even LeBron were on the same page, which is why fans had been so patient with the team, despite the Cavaliers playing in only one NBA Finals (2006–2007) since LeBron's arrival in 2003. When Gilbert, a shrewd businessman who loved sports, took over the team, Gilbert, Ferry, and Brown started to make well-thought-out and strategic moves. Before the 2006–07 season, the Cavaliers drafted Daniel

(above) Speedy guards like Daniel Gibson and Mo Williams give the Cavaliers a dynamic backcourt that helps spark LeBron James' creativity. (opposite) With loads of potential and a shooting touch that can't be taught, Daniel Gibson was one of the first players the team drafted truly to be a complement to LeBron. He has grown into his role over his brief career and could be poised for a breakout season.

"Boobie" Gibson, who came to the team from the University of Texas and gave them a solid point guard who could shoot. Gibson wasn't a starter at the beginning of the season, but he had talent and gave the Cavaliers a legitimate backcourt player with the potential to complement LeBron in the future.

Gibson gained valuable experience during his rookie season and scored a career-high 31 points in a 92–82 win at home against the Washington Wizards in the first-round series-clinching Game 6. The Cavaliers won their first Eastern Conference championship that season.

The next season (2007–2008), the Cavaliers acquired Delonte West and Wally Szczerbiak from the Seattle SuperSonics and Ben Wallace and Joe Smith from the Chicago Bulls. In exchange, the Cavaliers sent Larry Hughes, Drew Gooden, Cedric Simmons, and Shannon Brown to the Bulls and Ira Newble and Donyell Marshall to the Sonics.

It was a great deal for the Cavaliers because West and Szczerbiak helped the Cavaliers add depth and experience in the backcourt, while Wallace and Smith did the same thing for the front court. And with West and Szczerbiak, the Cavaliers now had backcourt players with outside scoring potential, especially with Szczerbiak's 3-point prowess. Slowly but surely, Ferry and Brown were building that NBA championship team.

Then in the 2008 offseason, the Cavaliers traded forward Joe Smith to Oklahoma City and point guard Damon Jones to the Milwaukee Bucks and acquired point guard Maurice "Mo" Williams from Milwaukee. Smith was a fan and organization favorite, while Jones had worn out his welcome. One local media personality, Kenny Roda, nicknamed Damon Jones, "Amon Ones" because he had no "D" (defense) and no "J" (jumpshot).

But later in that 2008 season, the Cavaliers reacquired Smith, who always performed admirably with the Cavaliers and was the ultimate professional when he was with Cleveland.

However, one of the biggest stories for the Cavaliers during the 2008–09 season was the play of Williams and West during the regular season. With those two players in the starting lineup, Cleveland had one of the best backcourts in the Eastern Conference. Williams was outstanding running the Cavaliers offense, but at the same time, he was a scoring threat. He averaged 17.3 points and 4.1 assists a game during the regular season and had a career-high 44 points on February 11, 2009, against Phoenix. He averaged 16.3 points and 4.1 assists in the playoffs.

West averaged 11.5 points a game during the regular season and 14.5 points during the playoffs.

As critical as Shaq and the newcomers are to the Cavaliers' shot at a world championship, West and Williams, the two smallest players on the team, may end up being crucial pieces to the puzzle.

But the centerpiece is one man: LeBron James. ■

One of the biggest surprises of 2008–2009 was the play of Delonte West, who had a terrific season.

52

All of the offseason moves have made the Cavaliers a force to be reckoned with in the NBA, but their fortunes still rest on the shoulders of their superstar. LeBron knows that it will take nothing less than 100 percent dedication to succeed in 2009-2010.

2008–2009: A Season of
HIGHS AND LOWS

With the type of regular season the Cavaliers had during 2008–2009, they were the favorites to represent the Eastern Conference and play for their first NBA championship.

Some highlights:

• Their 66–16 record was the winningest season in the franchise's history.

• They finished with a 39–2 record at home, which was just one game shy of the all-time franchise-best home record.

• Individual awards went to coach Mike Brown, who was named NBA Coach of the Year, while LeBron was named the league MVP and was second in the voting for Defensive Player of the Year.

• LeBron set the NBA record for most points in the first four games of a conference finals series

(169), breaking a mark that had just been set the same year by Kobe Bryant (147). The Cavaliers had all the momentum heading into the playoffs as the No. 1 seed and had home-court advantage throughout the playoffs.

The Cavaliers swept the Detroit Pistons 4–0 in the first round and won every game by 10 or more points. They did the same thing in the next round against the Atlanta Hawks and became the first team in NBA history to win eight straight playoff games by a double-digit margin.

But then came the Orlando Magic series in the Eastern Conference Finals. While the Cavaliers had dismantled their two opponents in the first two rounds, Orlando had struggled with Philadelphia and Boston but escaped both series. However, Magic center Dwight Howard, forwards Rashard Lewis and Hedo Turkoglu, guard Rafer Alston, and the rest of the squad regrouped for Cleveland, and Cavaliers fans were devastated after center Dwight

The Cavaliers were simply too much for the Detroit Pistons and Atlanta Hawks in the first two rounds of the playoffs. Their opponents went out with a whimper—eight straight losses, all by double digits.

Howard and the rest of the Orlando Magic disposed of the Cavaliers 4–2 in the Eastern Conference Finals.

Game 1 set the tone for the entire series. LeBron and the Cavaliers started out strong at home and even built a 16-point lead. That lead didn't hold up, and the Magic rallied back to stun the Cavaliers 107–106, despite a 49-point performance by LeBron. What was most demoralizing was the fact that Cleveland squandered a 16-point lead at home in the playoffs.

Yet, that wasn't anything new for the Cavaliers because during the regular season they would routinely take big leads, let a team battle back, and prevail in the end with LeBron, Mo, Delonte, or Z—but mostly LeBron—stepping up to help the Cavaliers prevail. It was a something Coach Mike Brown hated to see because he knew that once the playoffs started, there was no room for error.

Another thing the Cavaliers didn't want to admit after Game 1: the loss changed the entire series and shifted the momentum in Orlando's favor. It happened with just that one game. So Game 2 became a must-win for the Cavaliers.

It was a game similar to Game 1. The Cavaliers opened the game strong and built a comfortable 23-point lead. Then it happened. Cleveland couldn't hold on to the lead and found itself trailing 95–93 after Turkoglu hit a tough jumper in the lane with one second left. The Cavaliers couldn't afford to lose

(above) Despite building a 16-point lead in Game 1 at home against Orlando, the Cavaliers stumbled, losing a heartbreaker despite 49 points from LeBron. (opposite) After losing Game 1 at home, the Cavaliers knew that they needed to come out strong and earn at least a home split before the series moved to Florida. Again, however, they blew a big lead and trailed by two late.

another home playoff game. A loss here, and the series was over.

With hopes of pulling out a win slim to none, Mo Williams, standing almost near halfcourt, inbounded the ball to LeBron. TNT announcer Marv Albert's account: "With one second left…Rashard Lewis playing off the ball…(Williams) passing the ball in…LeBron drives into the key…near the foul line…just enough space to get back out to the top of the key outside the three-point line…he raises over (Turkoglu) and almost has to catch and shoot, no time to look at the basket…"

Just after LeBron released the ball, the horn sounded, the shot went in, and Albert continued: "LeBron James at the buzzer…as the Cavaliers have pulled it off to tie the series at 1–1 with one miraculous shot by James."

That shot was, and probably still will be, considered one of the greatest last-second shots in NBA playoffs history.

The shot even amazed the King.

"I just took my time. I just took my time," he said about the shot. "For me, a second is a long time. You know, for others it is very short. I mean, those are…as a kid, you practice those types of moments. As a basketball player, you are sitting in your backyard, you are in the gym, and you are five, four, three, two, one (buzzer sound). Those are the moments that as kids…you don't have to be in the

NBA to know what I'm talking about. Everybody knows those types of moments. And to hit a shot like that at the buzzer at home, wow."

What also amazed LeBron was the way the crowd erupted in jubilation after the shot. "Wow," he said once again. "I mean, the reaction from the fans and the teammates, the loudest it has ever been in this building was the first time I made the playoffs in my third year and we faced Washington and we ran out on the court on that game, the towels was out, and it was unbelievable. I had lost my wind as soon as I ran out on the court. (Tonight) surpassed that by ten times. I mean, it was unbelievable. I mean, you couldn't…I mean, you couldn't hear anything but just a roar of those 20,000-plus fans. And they deserve it. They deserve it."

LeBron was asked if his shot would finally put to rest all the talk and replays of Michael Jordan's game-winning shot against the Cavaliers in Game 5 of the first round of the 1989 playoffs at Richfield Coliseum. Jordan's buzzer-beater gave the Bulls a 116–115 win on Cleveland's home floor and knocked the Cavaliers out of the playoffs.

That play, in a long line of disheartening Cleveland sports lore, will forever be known as "The Shot."

"Well, that guy is not in the league anymore," LeBron said, referring to his idol, Michael Jordan. "The other 'three' is on the good side now. That

Immediately after his game-winning shot, LeBron stands triumphantly as he awaits the crush of his teammates. The noise in Quicken Loans Arena was deafening, leaving LeBron nearly speechless after the game except to say that it was the loudest he'd heard in his career up to that point.

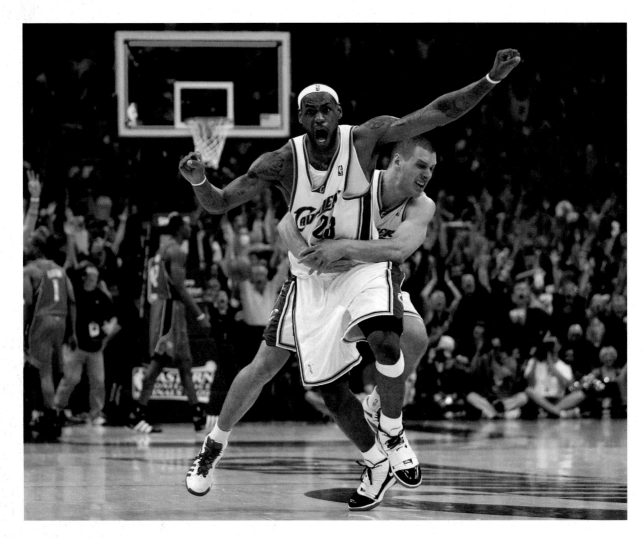

other 'three' is gone, so we don't have to worry about that no more."

Meanwhile, LeBron was asked if he was surprised he got open for the shot and if he thought the set confused Orlando's defense. "No," James said. "For one, I think they've seen that set before. We ran it one time earlier in the season in Indiana right before the All-Star break, and I was able to get a foul on Danny Granger. Rashard Lewis played it perfect. He stood tall, got in Mo's way, and dropped it. If you watch the replay, Rashard Lewis even got

a contest on the shot when I got up, but just a little bit too late. I mean, they played it perfect. It is just a good shot. It is a good shot. The same way we guard Rashard, when Rashard hit that three, we guarded it perfect. Good players or great players just make good shots."

Another question reporters asked was how that shot compared to the spectacular performance he put on a few years ago in the playoffs when he scored 25 points in the fourth quarter to help lift the Cavaliers over the Pistons. "I wouldn't say 'put one

(above) Sasha Pavlovic was the first Cavalier to make it to the jubilant James, wrapping him in a bear hug. The scene was magical, but the Magic would not lie down. For the moment, the series was tied and the Cavaliers had the momentum. (opposite) The gravity of the shot wasn't lost on James. He commented after the game that he was sure to see the clip again and again. The King wasn't the only one to believe it—commentators quickly rated it as one of the best buzzer-beaters in playoff history.

ahead of the other,'" LeBron said, understanding that although his game-winning shot was big, he still knew his team was in for a tough battle with the Magic. "That was a great performance also from us as a team, from me as an individual. (Tonight) was another good performance by me as an individual and us as a team.

"That's a shot that you will see for a long time, you know," LeBron continued. "You watch classic games, and you see Jordan hit game-winners, and you go all the way back, Jerry West hitting game-winners, and Magic Johnson going across the lane and hitting the jump hook against Boston. You see all these type of shots, man, they will always be played even when the game has left you as an individual. Hopefully I can stick my foot in that category with Magic and Jerry West and Jordan and all these other guys that made spectacular plays on the biggest stage in the world."

Was LeBron trying to put his name up there with some of the greats because of his game-winning shot?

"It's something I will probably do after I'm done playing the game of basketball," he humbly said. "I don't take time to look at what I do as an individual while I'm still playing this team game. When I'm done and retired, and I'm gone away from the game, I'm by myself, my family, my kids, I can look back on what I did as an individual. As long as I have 14 teammates, I will never look upon what I do as an individual. That's not how I approach the game."

Despite an outstanding individual performance by LeBron against Orlando in the playoffs, it wasn't enough. Orlando was too physical inside with Howard and on the perimeter with Lewis and Turkoglu, Orlando consistently shot over Cleveland's much smaller guards.

"That was our backbone all year," Wally Szczerbiak said about Cleveland's defense, "and we gave up 100 [points] every game except one. We couldn't find a way to stop these guys."

There wasn't much Cleveland could do during the series or say afterward. LeBron's game-winner had evened the series, but Orlando proved to be too much and knocked the Cavaliers out of the playoffs with a 103–90 win over Cleveland in Game 6 in Orlando.

"Our margin for error was very slim against this team," Szczerbiak told NBA.com's John Schuhmann, who covered the Eastern Conference Finals. "(Orlando) posed a lot of matchup problems for us, and they are playing at a very high level. We fought as hard as we could, and we just came up short."

Dwight Howard scored 40 points and had 14 rebounds in the decisive Game 6. He also made 70 percent of his free throws. Howard's inside presence and Orlando's pinpoint outside shooting ripped Cleveland's defense to shreds.

"They had a dominant big man, they were knocking down threes all over the floor, and they had our heads spinning in rotations the whole entire time,"

Orlando eventually proved to be too much. Their physical defense, combined with an offensive thrust that scored more than 100 points in five of the six games, ultimately did the Cavaliers in.

Szczerbiak told reporters. "It seemed like they shot 100 percent from the three the whole series," Mo Williams added.

Cavaliers coach Mike Brown couldn't mask his disappointment during the postgame interview because this was the team that many felt would be playing for an NBA championship.

"It was a tough night. It was disappointing," Brown said. "We had a heck of a season, but we had one goal in mind, and we came up short. You have to give the Magic credit. They were a tough opponent for us...they put Dwight Howard on the post, and we tried to double-team him, and when we double-teamed him, he did a heck of a job of passing out of the double-team, and their guys stepped up and made shots.

"And when we didn't double-team (Howard), he did a heck of a job scoring," Brown said. "Not only that, they rebounded. You have to give him credit. He was a monster (tonight). He had 40 points, and we threw a lot of different things at him. And he was patient and eight out of 10 times, if not more, he made the right play."

What also hurt the Cavaliers in the Orlando series was the inconsistent and ineffective shooting from Williams and Delonte West. After hitting 3-of-4 and 6-of-9 from three-point range in the first two games of the series, Williams was 6-of-27 in the remaining four games.

After the Cavaliers' loss in Game 6 in Orlando, LeBron walked off the court without congratulating

(above) In the end, the Cavaliers could only watch as the Magic finished them off to move on to the NBA Finals. It was a frustrating end to a season that many saw as the crowning moment for the franchise. (opposite) The Cavaliers made an effort to double-team Dwight Howard throughout the series, but they still struggled to contain him. Even when he was successfully trapped, Howard was often able to deftly pass out of it.

any of the Orlando players or shaking anyone's hand, which started a groundswell of criticism charging that LeBron was a prima donna who lacked sportsmanship and class. LeBron was obviously upset and disappointed in the outcome. And he didn't participate in the postgame press conference. He didn't talk to the media, period. For that, he was fined by the NBA.

Months later, in the summer of 2009, LeBron was speaking at the National Association of Black Journalists convention in Tampa and talked openly about that situation. He did have some remorse about not speaking to the media.

"I wouldn't have done it the same," James said at the convention. "I would have talked with the media. Looking back on it, without you guys, there's no LeBron James, Dwayne Wade, Tiger Woods, or no Peyton Manning."

He didn't have the same feelings about walking off the court and not shaking hands.

"Shaking hands is not a big deal to me," James said. "It's not being a sore loser; it's moving on. I look at the handshake like this: during the regular season, no one ever says anything. We play 82 regular-season games, eight preseason games, guys at the end of the game, no one ever shakes hands. Ever. And you move on to the next game. The congratulations, I congratulated Dwight (Howard) via email, told him congratulations and good luck in the finals. The shaking hands thing is really not a big thing for me. It's not I'm a sore

loser or anything like that. I'm just moving on. You guys beat me...I think sometimes people want you to accept losing, and I will never accept losing. There's ways to handle it certain times, and shaking hands may be it. But I will never accept losing, at anything that I do."

Then there was the big to-do about nothing—the video of LeBron being dunked on by Xavier University basketball player Jordan Crawford during LeBron's Skills Academy in Akron.

The tape was confiscated by Nike officials, which started a media frenzy.

"I never told anyone to confiscate any tapes," LeBron said. "Nike has a no-videotape policy at pickup games."

And looking back on the play, it wasn't that spectacular—at least it wasn't spectacular enough, in LeBron's opinion, to have been such a hot topic in the news for as long as it was.

"It's a play that happens in basketball all the time," he said. "You can go on YouTube and see me being dunked on by a lot of guys. I like to call myself a shot-blocker, and getting dunked on tends to happen."

More of LeBron's individual highlights from the 2008–2009 season:

• LeBron became the first player in Cavaliers franchise history to receive the MVP award after leading

A clearly frustrated LeBron James had a hard time swallowing the Orlando loss. A competitor to the core, he took some flak for not shaking hands after Game 6, but apologized over the summer for his actions.

the Cavaliers to an NBA- and franchise-best 66–16 (.805) record. He averaged 28.4 points, 7.6 rebounds, 7.2 assists, 1.69 steals, and a career-best 1.15 blocks in 37.7 minutes per game. The 6-foot-8 forward also posted career highs in games played (81), field-goal percentage (.489), and free throw percentage (.780). He was the only player in the NBA to average at least 28.0 points, 7.0 rebounds, and 7.0 assists per game this season. Leading the Cavs in points, rebounds, assists, steals, and blocks, James became just the fourth player since the 1973–74 season (when steals and blocks became official stats) to lead his team in each category.

• LeBron led the NBA in triple doubles (7), points per game in road games (31.5), and combined points, rebounds, and assists average (43.3). He ranked second in points per game (28.4) and total fourth-quarter points (515), eighth in steals (1.69), ninth in assists (7.2), tied for 14th in double doubles (29), 23rd in blocks (1.15), and 27th in rebounds (7.6).

• At 24 years, 106 days old, LeBron was the youngest player to win the MVP award since Moses Malone (24 years, 16 days) in 1978–79, and his 474-point margin of victory is the sixth-largest in MVP voting history (the media began voting during the 1980–81 season).

• During the season, LeBron was named Eastern Conference Player of the Week an all-time NBA-best seven times and tied the league record for most Player of the Month wins with four (November, January, March, and April). He was named an Eastern Conference All-Star starter for the fifth consecutive season and finished as runner-up to Orlando Magic center Dwight Howard for the NBA's Defensive Player of the Year.

One of LeBron's biggest thrills of the season was winning the MVP award and being able to hold the press conference at his high school with his family and friends from Akron. All of his Cavaliers teammates drove about 30 minutes from Cleveland to attend.

"To be voted Most Valuable Player is unbelievable," LeBron said. "People have been asking me, 'How does it feel?' And I don't know because it's an individual award. If you know me, individual accolades I never really get high on. This is a team award. Individual accolades come when team success is happening, and you look at those 14 guys over there, I got this award because of them because we put in the work before, during, and after practice."

LeBron was referring to all of his teammates sitting in the audience.

"We put in the work before, during, and after games," he said. "We put in the work every day, and people really don't see it. They just see the first, second, third, and fourth quarters. They really don't see that we get here an hour and a half before prac-

Under the banners at St. Vincent–St. Mary, LeBron accepts the 2009 NBA Most Valuable Player Award. He may be the cream of the crop in the NBA, but James has never forgotten where he came from. Every one of his teammates made the drive down to Akron to see him accept the award.

tice starts, and we don't leave until four hours after practice ends."

Cavaliers owner, Dan Gilbert, also was present at the press conference and spoke to what LeBron means to the organization, the community, and more.

"We all know that MVP stands for Most Valuable Player, and I think that we all know that there is really no doubt that LeBron James is the Most Valuable Player in the entire NBA, and the entire world, as far as we're concerned," Gilbert said. "But I think the 'P' in our view stands for 'Person'—Most Valuable Person—because LeBron James goes beyond a player. He really is to a lot of people a Most Valuable Person.

"This is a guy that not only gives to his teammates, he gives to his family, he gives to his friends, he gives to St. Vincent–St. Mary, he gives to Akron, he gives to the state of Ohio...he's given in so many more ways."

Mike Brown added: "More than a player, LeBron is a terrific person. In order to get to the level he's gotten to, you just can't be a great player. You just can't be the best player. You have to have something inside you that makes you a terrific human being, and that's what he is."

Winning the award and having his Cavaliers teammates with him meant a lot to LeBron. But to be honored right in the gym where he played with his high school and childhood friends was special.

"I wish my guys were here to be able to receive this award with me," LeBron said. "This is something we dreamed about as kids...winning the MVP of the NBA. As a kid growing up in Akron, you never think something like this could happen to you. You never think someone from Akron, Ohio, would be able to do the things we did growing up and do the things I'm trying to do as a basketball player and a person."

And naturally, LeBron thanked the lady that is most important in his life.

"My mother, Gloria James, is of course the reason I'm standing here," he said. "If any of you guys know my mother you know why these things have happened to me. Growing up, and for her being a single parent and financially nowhere near where we needed to be, and with me not having a father figure around to help me...I tell Savannah there's no way, even in the position I'm in today, that I would be able to raise LeBron by myself or raise Bryce by myself." (LeBron and his longtime girlfriend, Savannah, have two sons.)

"It couldn't happen. I don't know how (my mom) did it, and I still haven't figured it out. I'm in a lab working every day trying to figure out how you did it. I may be able to figure out how to hit a jumper or how to dunk the basketball, but I cannot figure out how you raised me by yourself. Wow." ∎

LeBron proudly hoists the MVP Award at a public celebration before the Cavaliers opened their playoff series with the Atlanta Hawks. In his discussions about winning the award, he is always quick to thank his mother, who raised him on her own and guided him down the right path.

A Remarkable (and Historical)
ROOKIE SEASON

There was no doubt about it: LeBron's rookie season in 2003–2004 was remarkable. With so much hype surrounding him, LeBron had to be spectacular in his first season, or he would've been called a bust. LeBron looked good during training camp and during preseason, but it wasn't the real thing. People wanted to see what he could do when it was "Showtime," a term made famous by Magic Johnson and the Los Angeles Lakers in the '80s.

So how did LeBron quiet his critics? He went out and won the NBA Rookie of the Year Award. He averaged 20.9 points, 5.5 rebounds, and 5.9 assists per game, joining Oscar Robertson and Michael Jordan as the only NBA rookies to average at least 20 points, five rebounds, and five assists. "They try to take away your manhood in this league, and they couldn't get mine," LeBron told members of the media as he received his trophy at the NBA store in New York from NBA Hall of Famer Julius "Dr. J" Erving. "I could have averaged around 25 points if I could have gotten a lot of calls."

Maybe. Still, Erving was impressed by LeBron's play during the 2003–2004 season. "I think nothing but extraordinary things about this extraordinary young man," Erving told reporters. "He silenced the critics early and often. This Rookie of the Year selection is his first step to going to the Basketball Hall of Fame."

The season before LeBron's arrival, the Cavaliers were 17–65, which tied for the worst record in the league. In LeBron's rookie season, Cleveland was 35–47 and finished ninth in the Eastern Conference, one spot out of the playoffs. James also helped home attendance rise from 11,497 to 18,288—the highest increase ever for a team that didn't move into a new building. "I knew I would make an impact this year," LeBron said. "And I guess I did." He received 508 points, including 78 of 118 possible first-place votes and was the first Cleveland rookie to win the award. Denver's

The first Cavalier to win the Rookie of the Year Award, LeBron easily outpaced Denver's Carmelo Anthony to win the honor. Not only did he turn around the fortunes of the Cavaliers on the court, but he also changed the mind-set of the entire franchise in just one season.

Carmelo Anthony was the runner-up. "People are going to think what they want to think," Anthony told reporters about finishing second. "I don't really know what else I could have done." Graciously, LeBron said, "I thought it could go either way. I thought it could be a split decision." Cavaliers Coach Paul Silas told the *San Diego Union-Tribune*: "He never hit the wall. He has that special body and a fine mind. Very seldom does the good Lord give a kid everything, like he gave Michael and LeBron."

The Cavaliers opened the regular season October 29, on the road against Sacramento and in front of a nationally televised audience on ESPN. There were all kinds of stars turning out to see "the Kid." A host of celebrities were on hand, as well as 350 members of the media, including some from Canada, Japan, and Taiwan. They all wanted to see if LeBron James was for real, if he was going to live up to the hype. Many wanted to see LeBron fail— fall flat on his face—so they could say, "See, we told you the kid wasn't ready to play with the big boys." Those detractors couldn't have been more wrong. They didn't know LeBron, where he came from, or what inspired him to be one of the best rookies to ever play the game. They soon found out when LeBron electrified the crowd, as he routinely did the entire season.

Despite the Cavaliers losing to Sacramento 106–92, it was instant success and instant stardom

(above) James tries to ignore the media blitz as he stretches before his first regular-season NBA game. The crowd in Sacramento and the millions watching on TV were anxious to see if "the Kid" was for real. (opposite) His 25-point performance under the glaring lights in his first game was notable but not as remarkable as James' absolute control of the game in front of him, showing the savvy of a seasoned veteran.

for LeBron. He finished with 25 points, nine assists, six rebounds, and four steals. "I could have helped my team a little bit more down the stretch," LeBron said after the game. "I could have been a little bit more aggressive to help us get the win."

As the *Desert Sun*, in Palms Spring, California, wrote after the game: "LeBron James more than lived up to his hype in the first regular-season game of his NBA career, playing like no other 18-year-old ever had in his professional debut...mesmerizing one of the league's loudest crowds with skills no teenager had ever displayed at this level." LeBron's agent, Aaron Goodwin, told the newspaper: "I think that was LeBron's statement to the league that he's here. He's for real." LeBron's point total was the most by any player who went from high school to the NBA. "This is the biggest regular-season game we've ever had here," said Joe Maloof to reporters. Maloof's family owns the Kings. "There was a buzz around the city. It doesn't get better than this. This is great for the league. We all need him. He's a breath of fresh air."

Back in Akron, LeBron's longtime friend, classmate, and teammate, Brandon Weems, and other close friends and teammates, were absolutely amazed. LeBron's high school buddies all gathered at the Weems' home—one of LeBron's homes-away-from-home as a kid—and reveled in LeBron's outstanding performance. "We knew LeBron could play in the NBA, and we knew he would hold his own, but I honestly didn't think he would do that well," Brandon said about LeBron's performance in Sacramento. "He was great. We should've known he would play well, because he always plays well under pressure."

At the same time, Brandon and his buddies didn't see a change in LeBron at all, when it came to hanging out with this NBA phenom. Because LeBron was still underage during his rookie season, he couldn't go out to bars and "kick it" with his older teammates at home or on the road. But it wasn't like LeBron wanted to do that anyway. He loved the fact that he was doing his thing in the NBA right there in Cleveland, 30 minutes from Akron.

On draft day of his senior year, when the Cavaliers had the most luck in the world in gaining the No. 1 pick, LeBron hosted a party at a downtown hotel in Akron for his friends and family. When he was officially drafted by the Cavaliers, he told anyone who would listen that he would "light up Cleveland like Las Vegas."

Weems said that during LeBron's rookie season, LeBron would "set us up" with season tickets for home games. After every home game, Weems and his buddies would leave the arena and go to LeBron's downtown apartment. It was a nice apartment by most standards, but it wasn't extravagant. LeBron wasn't like that. All he wanted to do after a

---

Being a young superstar and playing so close to home did not faze LeBron in his early days in the NBA. He was more than happy to participate in the community—here taking part in a turkey giveaway at Thanksgiving. After games, he was content to retire to his apartment and play video games with friends.

home game was go back to his apartment, meet up with his friends, and have a PlayStation tournament.

"LeBron thought he was all that, but we used to tear him up," Weems bragged. LeBron never admitted to that.

Weems also revealed LeBron's sense of humor. Weems said that when they would be at LeBron's apartment waiting for him after a home game, they would drink all of his Sprite that was in the refrigerator. At the time, LeBron had a contract with Sprite. One day, LeBron came home from a game and noticed that most of the Sprite in his refrigerator was gone.

So LeBron, being LeBron, played a joke on his buddies.

"LeBron had a chef, so when we went to see him we could eat anything we wanted," Weems said. But one time, we went into the kitchen to get something to drink, and he had a Sprite machine put in. We had to pay 50 cents to get a pop. He thought that was hilarious."

Meanwhile, on the court LeBron was so impressive during his first year in the NBA that he was named Rookie of the Month in the Eastern Conference every month of the season—seven consecutive months—which was incredible. But to give

(above) There was no doubt about who the best rookies in the NBA were in 2003–2004. LeBron and Carmelo Anthony won their conference's Rookie of the Month award every time they were given. (opposite) The comparisons had been going on for several years by the time both players reached the NBA. LeBron was very gracious when he was named Rookie of the Year, complimenting Anthony and saying that he thought the race was going to be very close.

Carmelo Anthony credit, he was named the Western Conference Rookie of the Year each month of the season. The rivalry that began at the high school level between these two future NBA superstars continued into their rookie seasons.

As the season progressed, it was apparent that LeBron was the real deal. In his rookie season, he played in 79 games, starting in every contest. His impressive scoring, rebounding, and assist stats earned him NBA Rookie of the Year honors. On February 9, 2004, he became the youngest player in NBA history to score 1,000 points and the youngest to score 40 points in a game on March 27 when he scored 41 against the New Jersey Nets. (He also doled out 13 assists in that contest.) The biggest negative of James' rookie campaign was missing three consecutive games with a sprained right ankle (January 20–24).

What was also impressive was the fact that LeBron was helping to lead and transform a team that had tied for the worst record in the league the previous season into one that was making a run at the playoffs. And credit the Cavaliers organization for making early season moves to surround LeBron with the right mix of players to make the team successful. They traded Ricky Davis, a selfish player on the court but friendly person off the court. In return, they got forward/center Tony Battie and forward Eric Williams. The Cavaliers also traded to Portland Darius Miles, who went from high school straight to the NBA a few years before LeBron did the same. That trade was probably the most important for the Cavaliers during the year. In return for Miles, Cleveland received point guard Jeff McInnis, who was extremely effective in running the offense and allowing LeBron to play more of the shooting guard and small forward positions. The addition of the new players made the Cavaliers a playoff contender, even though they failed to make the postseason by one game.

LeBron's debut at the famed Madison Square Garden in New York City was a hit. And it was obvious that New Yorkers were anxiously awaiting the game on February 22, 2004. There it was: a four-story billboard of LeBron on Seventh Avenue just a block from the Garden. The billboard didn't sit well with Knicks players. The only thing they could do was get their revenge on the court. It didn't happen. LeBron scored 22 points in a 92–86 win in front of a sellout crowd. A few nights earlier, LeBron scored 32 points in a win against San Antonio. What did LeBron think about his performance in New York? "A good basketball player, this is one arena you want to play in," he said after the game.

LeBron did experience some adversity after suffering an ankle injury on January 17, 2004, at Utah in the Cavaliers' 40th game of an 82-game regular season. As Cavaliers fans held their collective

The New York Knicks were motivated to slow down LeBron by the four-story billboard of the Cleveland star in Times Square, but they could not contain even a hobbled James in the Cavs' 92–86 win.

In one of his finest performances of his rookie year, LeBron scored 32 points against San Antonio, one of the toughest defenses in the NBA.

breaths fearing the worst—that their savior was going to be lost for the season—they were relieved to know that the injury wasn't season ending. LeBron missed just a few games. But to illustrate just how loyal LeBron was to his friends and family and former teammates at St. Vincent–St. Mary, consider this. LeBron injured his ankle on a Saturday in Utah. The team flew across the country back to Cleveland that night. St. Vincent–St. Mary was playing a high school game Sunday afternoon. It was a regular occurrence for LeBron to attend his old high school games when the Cavaliers were in town, but no one expected him to be at this particular game, especially after his injury. But there was LeBron, hobbling down the steps at the University of Akron's James A. Rhodes Arena, where the game was being played, on crutches and needing assistance just to maneuver to his seat. Why in the world did LeBron attend that game after injuring his ankle less than 24 hours earlier? Simple. LeBron was being LeBron, and he wanted to be there for his friends like they had always been there for him.

Several months later, back at 100 percent, LeBron made history. On March 27, he scored 41 points against New Jersey to become the youngest player in league history to break 40. He scored more than 30 points 13 times. There were many other firsts for LeBron during his rookie season. He was the first high school player who went straight to the NBA to score 25 points in his pro debut, the

(above) Despite hurting his ankle in Salt Lake City against the Jazz, LeBron showed his commitment to his alma mater by attending a St. Vincent–St. Mary's game just 24 hours later in Akron. (opposite) LeBron's prodigious scoring in his rookie year helped him set several NBA records, including his March game against New Jersey that made him the youngest player to ever score 40 points in a game.

youngest player to score 40 points in a game, and the youngest player to score 1,000 career points.

As impressive as his on-court accomplishments were his endorsement deals. As part of his six-year multimillion dollar deal with Coca-Cola, LeBron helped develop Flava23, a red sourberry flavor for his own Powerade beverage. In a release sent out via email, LeBron said he "picked a color close to the Cavaliers' road jersey. I chose sourberry because I like the fruity taste." For Coca-Cola, it was a fruitful deal. "Most brands would think it's a risk," said Mary Herrera, director of sports and energy drinks for Coke in North America. "It's not about being perfect. It's about challenging convention. LeBron was perfect for this." A comic book concept was developed where LeBron appeared in 3 million copies of *King James* by DC Comics. Powerade shows up when James takes on tough street-ball players. "I grew up reading comic books," LeBron said. "I want my character to grow into a Batman/Bruce Wayne type, a regular guy who helps people and makes the world a better place." Then there were Nike's ads for LeBron's second shoe—Zoom LeBron II—that was released in November 2005. He also signed a five-year deal in July 2004 with Bubblicious gum.

LeBron became an icon in just his first year in the NBA, and everybody wanted a piece of him—from the corporations, to the media, to the fans. "It was the most unbelievable media blitz and scrutiny

I've seen in my 35-plus years in the league," Coach Silas told the *San Diego Union-Tribune*. "I've never seen anything like it. It was mayhem at times. With the kids, especially. We'd get to hotels at 2:00 in the morning and there would be 30 to 40 kids waiting for LeBron's autograph. When we got to Philadelphia, we were let off down below, and the fans couldn't get to us. They were up on top of the ramp looking over as we got off the bus. They were lowering LeBron James jerseys on ropes for him to autograph. They were ingenious."

With so much attention paid to LeBron and the Cavaliers, many players around the league expressed interest in playing for Cleveland. Former Cavaliers forward Carlos Boozer and LeBron were outstanding together, and it was expected that the two would play together in Cleveland for years, possibly leading the organization to a long-awaited NBA title. But the two players played together just one season—LeBron's rookie year. In a "contract dispute," Boozer left Cleveland after the 2003–2004 season and signed a deal with the Utah Jazz that paid him more than $60 million. LeBron was disappointed that he would no longer have the chance to play with Boozer in Cleveland but showed support for his friend and former teammate. "It hurts us, of course," he told *Akron Beacon Journal* reporter R.D. Heldenfels. "Everyone knows...even if you don't cover basketball, it really hurts us to lose a player like that. I'm great friends

In their lone season together, LeBron and Carlos Boozer showed a flair and chemistry that helped attract free agents to Cleveland—though Boozer was off to Utah in the summer of 2004.

with Carlos. We had a great run in the one year that I had him.... But he (has) got to do his best...for his family. As a person and as a man, I gotta respect that. It's a situation where his family comes first. People in your family come first before anybody—teammates, coaches, the NBA." Boozer, who once *was* one of Cleveland's fan favorites, instantly turned into one of the most disliked athletes to ever play in Cleveland. Fans felt betrayed. Meanwhile, Boozer talked about his relationship with LeBron. "Well, it was great playing with LeBron. We both helped each other a lot. I was more of a big brother to him, and we got almost everything we could have. We almost made the playoffs together. Stuff like that happens. It's a business decision, and at the same time it was an individual decision."

The two players did get a chance to play on the same team before Boozer went to Utah. It was in Athens, Greece, for the 2004 Summer Olympic Games. The two were on Team USA—a squad expected to win the gold medal easily. Instead, Team USA was a big disappointment, having to settle for the bronze medal. It was the first American squad not to take the Olympic title since NBA players were eligible in 1992. LeBron, who played sparingly in Athens, wasn't the star of the team like he was in the NBA. But when he did play, he provided energy. In fact, Team USA outscored its opponents in the combined time LeBron was in the game. Boozer was average. The entire team was average. LeBron and Carmelo, two of the youngest players on the team, never could get into a rhythm because they didn't play extended amounts of minutes.

"It's probably been the hardest for Carmelo

(above) Despite a roster dotted with current stars like Tim Duncan, young up-and-comers like Carmelo Anthony and LeBron James, and role players like Carlos Boozer, Team USA was able to win only bronze in Athens. (opposite) LeBron did not play a starring role for the Red, White, and Blue, but he was effective in the international game, statistically making Team USA better every time he was on the floor.

and LeBron because of all the hype," said Team USA coach Larry Brown, who guided the Detroit Pistons to an NBA championship that same year. "They've always started and been the stars, always been the focal points, and it's been a real terrible adjustment—a difficult adjustment—for both of them. They had no clue. The idea was to get young kids that would sit and learn and be the future of our Olympic team, and it's been very hard for them to figure that out." LeBron acknowledged that the Olympics were a learning experience. "I had no idea what I was getting into," he told reporters. "This is the Olympic team. I just wanted to be on the Olympic team and have the experience. Everything on the court I did not expect, but I think I'd do it again." George Karl, former Cavs and current Nuggets head coach, said in an ESPN report: "I tip my hat to LeBron just for being on the U.S. team. He gave up his summer to represent his country. He participated, and he played hard. That's enough, in my book."

LeBron was humbled by the experience and enjoyed his time playing international competition.

"To see other parts of the world matures you," he said just after the 2004 Olympics. "You see so much. You see in different countries how people struggle and how people grow up. I'm more of a better person and player than I was. It's been such a great experience, fighting for my country and laying it on the line. It's one of the best experiences I've ever had."

In 2008, the Summer Olympics were held in Beijing, China, and LeBron and the rest of Team USA had a completely different focus. LeBron wasn't even thinking about just being content that he was on the team. He didn't take being on the team for granted, but LeBron and Team USA had unfinished business to take care of in international play. Winning the bronze medal in 2004 was humiliating for Team USA.

When the 2008 Olympics rolled around, LeBron was one of the best players in the world, and he made sure he stood head and shoulders above the rest, as far as being a leader on Team USA. He spoke of his leadership role to the *New York Times*: "I knew it had to come from someone. It doesn't matter how good individuals are, if you don't have a leader, it's not going to be right. I took that responsibility from Day 1, saying I'm going to be the vocal leader, and I'm going to be the leader of this team."

Once the Games began, Team USA began knocking off teams, one after another. On August 24, Day 16 of the 2008 Olympic Games, LeBron and Team USA defeated Spain 118–107 to win the gold medal. Not long afterward, LeBron stood with teammates Michael Redd, Deron Williams, and Jason Kidd on the podium during the national anthem with their right hands across their hearts proudly wearing their gold medals.

LeBron later said it was the proudest moment of his professional career. ■

His first experience in international competition helped LeBron mature as a player, and he was happy to represent his country again in 2008. This time, there was plenty to smile about when he helped lead Team USA to the gold.

James has called winning in Beijing the proudest moment of his professional career. Showing off their medals, LeBron and other Team USA stars surround USA Basketball national director Jerry Colangelo at the medal ceremony.

The Making of the Movie
MORE THAN A GAME

More Than a Game. The title says it all. It's the critically acclaimed movie based on the lives of LeBron and his four childhood buddies, dubbed the "Fab Five." Along with LeBron, the rest of the group included "Little" Dru Joyce, Sian Cotton, Willie McGee, and Romeo Travis.

Meanwhile, young Akron native Kristopher Belman never knew his life would change forever with one idea that came to mind while he was a film student at Loyola Marymount University in Los Angeles. During Belman's senior year at Loyola Marymount, one of his required assignments for graduation was to do a 12- to 15-minute documentary.

Belman wasn't sure what he would do. Before he left Los Angeles for his parents' home in Akron for Thanksgiving break, Belman often heard friends in Los Angeles talk about LeBron James. And they realized that LeBron was from Belman's hometown.

Belman never gave it any thought until he got back to Akron. He saw firsthand the buzz that surrounded LeBron in Akron, around Northeast Ohio, and all over the state.

But as Belman started to take in the atmosphere in Akron and notice how people were enamored by LeBron, he realized that it wasn't just about LeBron James. The St. Vincent–St. Mary team was just that—a team—and the success the Irish had in the past and was having at the time had everything to do with the entire team, not just LeBron.

That's when it hit Belman. He knew exactly what his project would be. He was going to do a documentary on the Fab Five. Belman went to St–Vincent-St. Mary headmaster, Dave Rathz, and head coach, Dru Joyce, and explained what he wanted to do.

Up to that point, Rathz, Joyce, and the rest of the St. Vincent–St. Mary community had been apprehensive about allowing journalists near the team. In fact, practices were closed, for the most part, because the season, which was just in its first or second month, had become a media circus.

It wasn't unusual to ride by the school at the top of the hill on Maple Street and see television trucks,

The Irish offense may have gone through LeBron James, but it was teammates like Romeo Travis, part of the St. Vincent–St. Mary "Fab Five," that enabled the team to have such incredible success.

The story of *More Than a Game* is about the bond of brotherhood that the young players, including James, formed through years of playing together.

with antennas reaching high into the sky. Belman convinced officials at St. Vincent–St. Mary that he wasn't trying to exploit LeBron, the team, or the school. He explained that he was a fellow Akronite who was off at film school and was just hoping to put together a meaningful project that would positively reflect his hometown.

From around Christmas of LeBron's senior year until graduation, Belman got complete and total access to the team. He was in the locker room before games, after games, and during practices. He rode the bus to and from games, always filming. He went out to eat with LeBron and the players when they were just being high school kids.

He simply became known as "Camera Man"

and not Kris. Belman gained the trust of LeBron and the team, and as a result, his project was a hit. But it was such a hit that he continued to work on the project after graduation. With the cooperation of LeBron and LeBron's close childhood friend and now business partner, Maverick Carter, they decided to make Belman's senior project into a full-length feature film. LeBron and Maverick became executive producers.

Belman used old footage of the young boys playing in AAU tournaments as well as private home movies to give the film a personal touch. There also is extensive footage of LeBron and his teammates during their four years in high school. On September 6, 2008, Belman's film premiered at

(above) LeBron, Dru Joyce III and Sian Cotton reunite in their old stomping grounds, the gym at St. Vincent–St. Mary, to promote *More Than a Game*. (opposite) School administrators along with Fighting Irish head coach Dru Joyce II allowed Kris Belman unparalleled access to the team. He opened up practices and even allowed Belman into the locker room and on the team bus.

the Toronto International Film Festival. Some of the other films that debuted at the film festival were *Burn After Reading*, starring George Clooney and Brad Pitt, and Spike Lee's *Miracle at St. Ann*. In fact, after the premiere of *More Than a Game*, LeBron held a private, invitation-only dinner at a very nice restaurant in downtown Toronto, and Spike Lee was one of the guests. Then, after the dinner, there was an after-party for LeBron. Among the guests were Jennifer Hudson, Queen Latifah, Alicia Keys, and singer Robin Thicke, who even performed a few songs.

The audience inside Ryerson Theater, which included more than 1,200 people, watched a powerful, emotional, and personal story about the lives of these young men. At the end of the film, the audience gave almost a five-minute standing ovation. Then, Belman, LeBron, and four of the five cast members went on stage for a question-and-answer session.

LeBron was the first to speak.

"I told myself that I wouldn't cry," LeBron said, pausing to gather his feelings and emotions. "This is the first time I've cried because of basketball or anything since we lost the national championship in the eighth grade."

LeBron, on stage after the film with his teammates, continued.

"On behalf of Romeo, Dru, Willie, and Coach Dru...this thing is authentic. Nothing you seen was scripted. You have reality shows these days where it

(above) The members of the "Fab Five" came back together for the September 2009 debut of *More Than a Game* in Toronto. The movie was acclaimed by the audience and critics alike for its fantastic take on a year in the lives of the young men. (opposite) Despite having the odds stacked against him, LeBron worked hard on the floor, leaned on his supporters and rose above his disadvantaged background. He credited basketball, but made a point of mentioning that any kid can use any outlet to rise above his or her challenging circumstances.

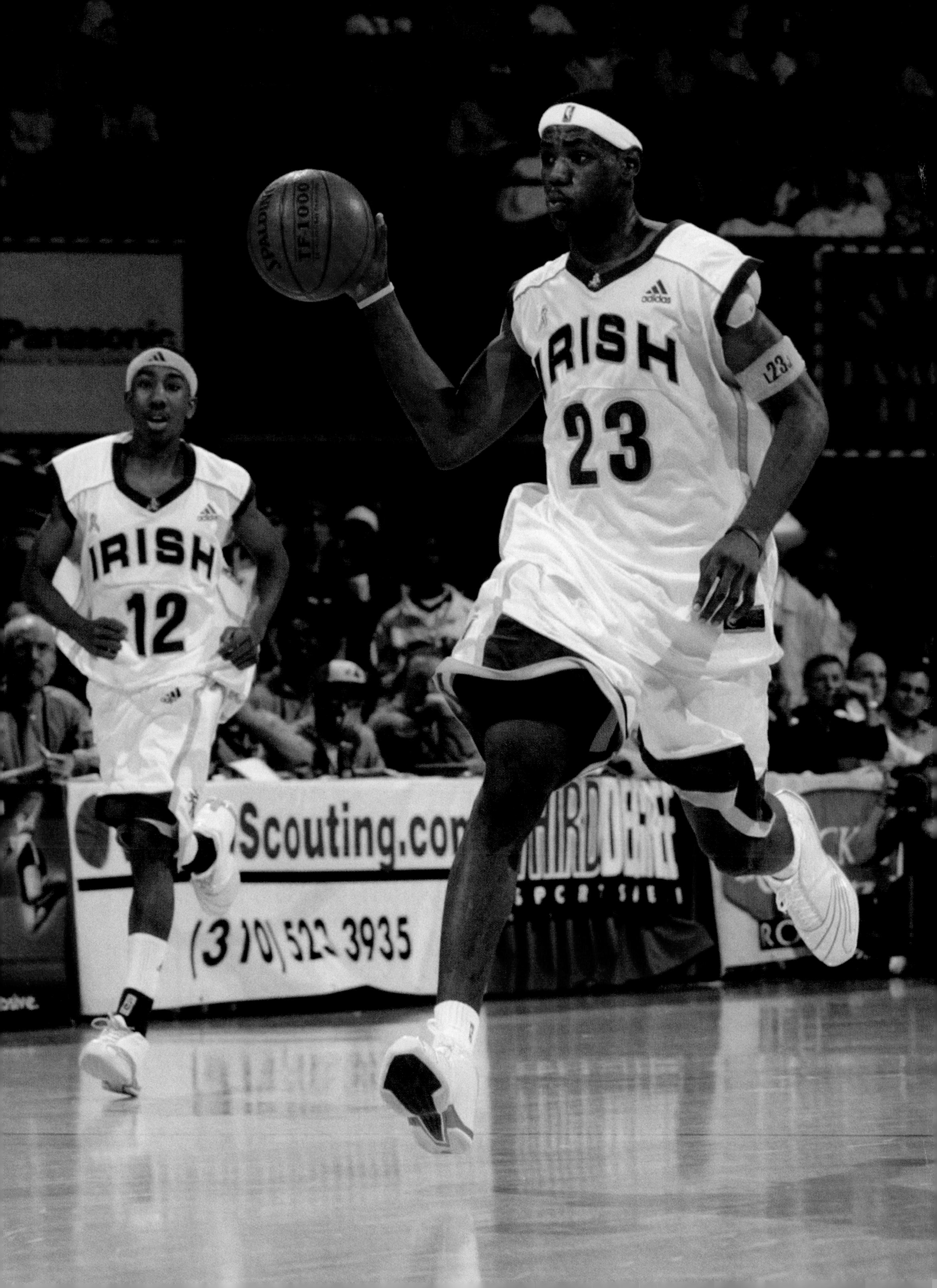
IRISH
23
IRISH
12
Scouting.com

may look like it's authentic, but most of them are scripted. They'll tell you, 'OK, we're going to go to the grocery store, and we want you to act a fool today.' We acted a fool on our own, and we told Kris to just run the tape."

The audience broke up in laughter.

Then, LeBron continued to reflect on what the film and what basketball meant to him and his friends.

"Basketball was the tool," he said. "It's more than basketball. It's coaches, parents, brothers, and sisters. We grew greatly by using the game of basketball, but it could be any sport. It could be any job. It could be anything where you could build a strong friendship and seek out to do bigger and bet-

ter things throughout your whole life."

If you really had a chance to spend time with LeBron from his childhood days, you could understand what friendship meant to him. Because he had such a rough childhood—being raised by a single mother who gave birth to LeBron when she was only 16—LeBron had the odds stacked against him. He was considered an at-risk kid, and he could've ended up in jail, on drugs, or much worse because of the unstable environment he was raised in. But he made basketball his love, and his teammates became his friends and family. That's why friendship always played an important part in LeBron's life, even as he made his ascension into the NBA.

"Leaving middle school, we could've split up,"

(above) Although he had the best access, Kris Belman's camera was far from the only one following LeBron James throughout his senior season at St. Vincent–St. Mary. No one else, however, better recorded the true essence of the now-legendary team. (opposite) Friendship with those who have stayed beside him through the years is an important part of LeBron's life. Growing up and playing basketball with the same group of kids provided a much-needed stability and purpose for the young King.

Willie McGee sits with LeBron in the gym at St. Vincent-St. Mary. The Fab Five have taken their own paths in life, with Dru Joyce and Romeo Travis playing professional ball in Europe and Sian Cotton playing college football, but they have become men shaped by their experiences playing together as boys.

LeBron said. "But once again, our friendship came into play. When Dru said, 'I'm not going (to school) here,' we said, 'OK, we're following you.'"

LeBron was referring to the fact that Little Dru wanted to go to St. Vincent–St. Mary instead of the public, urban school that was in his district. Little Dru's dad, Dru Joyce II, was an assistant coach at nearby Buchtel High School, a predominately black school, and even though Little Dru's dad was on the coaching staff, he felt he wouldn't get a chance to play there because of his size.

A few years earlier, Little Dru had struck up a friendship with Keith Dambrot, a short man and former college coach who has was running a basket-ball camp at the Akron Jewish Community Center. The two related to each other because they had gone through the same experiences as kids because of their size. A few years later, Dambrot got the head coaching job at St. Vincent–St. Mary, and when he did, Little Dru knew exactly where he was going to play. That decision changed so many people's lives forever.

The Fab Five had one of the most memorable four-year runs in high school basketball history.

"After graduating high school, we could've all said, 'It's been fun. I'm going to go on to the Cleveland Cavaliers, do my thing, and good luck with the rest of your lives.' It's not about that," LeBron said.

(above) There's plenty to smile about these days for LeBron, as he sits and laughs during an interview for *More Than a Game*. Kris Belman had done such a good job with his original student project that all the major players were eager to participate in the full documentary. (opposite) Even though LeBron was going to be the star of the show, it was Dru Joyce III who keyed the Fab Five's decision to go to St. Vincent–St. Mary. The boys chose to not split up for high school and Little Dru's dad was able to catch on with the Fighting Irish as a coach.

And just how important was the premiere for LeBron and his friends? Well, Little Dru and Romeo Travis flew in from Germany, where they were playing professionally. But LeBron wasn't about to let them overshadow him.

"Dru and Romeo flew in yesterday all the way from Germany on a nine-hour flight," LeBron said, as the crowd applauded. Then LeBron continued: "It doesn't compare to the 17-hour flight from Beijing (I took) back home (after the 2008 Olympics), but I give them credit."

The crowd laughed.

LeBron introduced friend and teammate Willie McGee, who, like so many others, drove six hours from Akron to Toronto for the event. Before LeBron introduced Coach Dru, the man who cared for all of those young men like they were his sons, he poured out his heart about how he felt about Coach Dru.

"You never know what life has in store for you, and I'm echoing Coach Dru's words," LeBron said. "You never know what life has in store for you until you go through it, and you look back on it, and you look back at the people who made every day possible for you. Coach Dru, being a father figure to me, being a father figure to Romeo and Willie, and of course being Dru's father, he gave us direction on becoming who we are today.

"We didn't know that Coach Dru was setting us

(above) Pictured on their high school senior night, the Fab Five came from far and wide to make it to Toronto for the premiere of *More Than a Game.* (opposite) No man got more praise during the premiere than coach Dru Joyce II. LeBron credited him with being a father figure and being one of the biggest influences on him during his adolescent years.

up to be the men we are at 22 and 23 years old," LeBron said. "At 14 and 15 years old, you can't look that far, but the more that you look back on the whole situation," (LeBron paused to once again gather his emotions), "it's unbelieveable. Thank you Coach Dru. Thank you."

Coach Dru couldn't help but get emotional. At that moment, he pulled out a tissue from his front pocket, dabbed the tears from his eyes, and wiped his nose.

Then, in typical fashion, Coach Dru spoke softly, and every word was heartfelt and meaningful.

"I just started out (coaching) as a dad, like any dad," he said. "I just happened to be blessed to just run into some guys that were pretty good. All this means to me is the job we did. Coach (Lee) Cotton, Coach Dambrot, we just believed that if you set a positive example and you raise a high standard, most kids will go to that standard, wherever you set the bar. So we just kept the bar high, always. I'm proud of them. They have gone far beyond what I thought. I was just trying to get them into college and help get them through those days of their lives."

Coach Dru paused to wipe his nose and tears again, then continued: "If they ever took anything from me, I hope it's what I took from the men who helped me, and it was to just give back, which I am hoping that they continue to do, give back."

(above) Director Kris Belman sits for an interview in the St. Vincent–St. Mary locker room in 2009. He discussed the experience of being around the young players when they were teens and then following up with them years later to complete the documentary. (opposite) There are few coaches who wear their hearts on their sleeves more than Keith Dambrot. He helped lead the Fighting Irish through their early successes and was aided every step of the way by Dru Joyce II and Lee Cotton.

The film isn't a story just about LeBron. It's a story about friendship and young boys coming together through basketball. It's about their camaraderie and these young boys learning about love, life, family, and responsibility first, then basketball second, carrying everything they learned into adulthood.

But long before LeBron hit the silver screen with *More Than a Game*, long before the appearances on the ESPY Awards, long before the appearances on *Saturday Night Live*, and long before the series of entertaining, inspirational, and humorous Nike commercials, LeBron had that *star* quality on and off the basketball court.

His charismatic charm and dazzling basketball skills started to develop around the age of eight. Actually, it started even before that, when LeBron was about three years old. One Christmas, his mother, Gloria—who had just one child, LeBron, at age 16—bought him a Nerf basketball hoop. Gloria said she "always had to keep raising the darn thing up because he was dunking on it back then."

But it was around the age of eight that LeBron's talent started to rise above the rest of his peers, and it never stopped rising. By the time LeBron was in high school at Akron's St. Vincent-St. Mary, playing with the same close friends he had played with on youth AAU basketball teams for years, they were the talk of the high school basketball universe. The hoops epicenter wasn't New

(above) Akron remains proud of its sons, as this theater marquee shows. *More Than a Game* is a film about much more than just LeBron James. (opposite) It was clear from a young age that LeBron was going to be special on the basketball court, but it wasn't until his time at St. Vincent–St. Mary that he turned his talent into superstardom.

York, Texas, or Florida. It was Akron, a city of about 220,000 people.

LeBron and the Fab Five were steamrolling opponents their senior year, trying to win a national championship that they failed to win when they were in the eighth grade. At that time, LeBron's Shooting Stars came from nowhere and methodically beat some of the best eighth-grade teams in the country during the tournament to reach the national championship game.

In the first half of the championship game, the Shooting Stars looked intimidated and out of synch. But in the second half, LeBron and his teammates regrouped and slowly made a comeback. The game came down to the final seconds and the last shot. LeBron's desperation shot at the buzzer rolled in and out, and his team lost by two points. They were devastated.

From that moment on, LeBron and his closest friends on that team decided they were going to high school together, with the sole goal of working hard for four years to get that opportunity to not only play for a high school national championship, but to win the national championship.

LeBron and St. Vincent–St. Mary traveled all over the country during his senior year, playing teams in Philadelphia at the famed Palestra, playing at UCLA's Pauley Pavilion, Mellon Arena in

(above) Basketball's biggest household name does not hail from the big city of New York or the playgrounds of Chicago—he comes from humble blue-collar roots in Akron, Ohio. (opposite) Even as LeBron quickly established himself as one of the best young players in the country, his friends and teammates were always right behind him.

Pittsburgh, the Wolstein Center in Cleveland, and the Greensboro Coliseum.

The journey for these young men ended at Ohio State University's Value City Arena and the Schottenstein Center, site of the Division II state championship. The Irish were facing Archbishop Kettering Alter for a chance at winning a third state championship in four years.

But for LeBron and his teammates, especially Dru, Sian, Willie, and Romeo, there was more at stake than just a state championship. That elusive national championship, which had been their goal since the eighth grade, was now within reach once again, thanks to the annual season-ending national rankings issued by *USA Today*. All they needed to do was win one more game to solidify their lock on the top spot in the poll and the plan from their freshman year would be complete. They had been preparing for this day ever since they lost in Orlando, and they knew this was the last chance in their lives that they would get another shot at a national championship.

Behind 25 points and 11 rebounds from LeBron, the Irish defeated Kettering Alter 40–36 for the state—and national—championship.

For the Fab Five, it was the sweetest victory that they had ever experienced in their young lives. ■

(above) Even with the cameras and bright spotlight of the national media on him, LeBron knew that a third state championship in four years was the ultimate goal. (opposite) Brandon Weems and the rest of the Fighting Irish knew they had a shot at winning a national championship. Their third state title in four years solidified their spot in the eyes of the *USA Today* and capped the run of one of the most dominant high school teams of all time.

Steve Urkel (Jaleel White): Cooler than You Think

When LeBron and St. Vincent–St. Mary went out to Los Angeles to play in the January 2004 Pangos Dream Classic at UCLA's legendary Pauley Pavillon, the hype surrounding the game was incredible. St. Vincent–St. Mary defeated Mater Dei 64–58 in a game that was televised by ESPN2 with former UCLA and NBA great Bill Walton on the announcing crew. But for me, the press luncheon the day before at famed Lawry's The Prime Rib in Beverly Hills was amazing. *Los Angeles Times* staff writer Ben Bolch summed it up best in a story about the tournament with the headline "It Brings Feast Fit for a King":

It was a luncheon fit for a head of state. The guests ate prime rib, mashed potatoes, creamed spinach, and Yorkshire pudding served from stainless-steel push carts while sitting in a finely appointed dining room. The obsequious hosts delivered the requisite podium joke and piled on the praise. There was even free limousine service available afterward.

All this, to honor a high school basketball player.

The luncheon Friday at Lawry's in Beverly Hills was ostensibly held to recognize the eight teams playing in the Pangos Dream Classic today at Pauley Pavillon. But it probably wouldn't have been held—and certainly at not such an opulent venue—without LeBron James.

It was at the luncheon that I had my brush with a celebrity. After we ate, the press conference began.

As LeBron and his teammates fielded questions, I could feel someone over my shoulder. So I turned around and just a few steps away was actor Jaleel White, "Steve Urkel" from the television show *Family Matters.*

I was absolutely shocked—not that I had just seen "Urkel," but at how normal and "un-Urkel" Jaleel looked. So after the luncheon we chatted and he told me that he had always been a basketball fan and that he had followed the Pangos Dream Classic for years because he always wanted to see the new, up-and-coming high school stars from across the country. And he had heard all about LeBron and the Irish and he wanted to see the phenom.

As we talked basketball—everything from Dr. J and Michael Jordan to LeBron—White told me he always loved the game and that he played in any kind of celebrity/charity basketball games he could. Then he asked, "Do you know of any good basketball books you can recommend?" I said, "Actually, I am writing a book right now about LeBron."

Jaleel was excited and we exchanged numbers. He said, "When the book comes out, please call me because I'd love to get one." Unfortunately, with all the hustle and bustle and distractions that were going on surrounding the game in Los Angeles, I lost his business card. We were never able to reconnect, but it was really nice meeting him.

LOS ANGELES

Dealing with Tough Questions

After St. Vincent–St. Mary defeated Mater Dei, I remember a tense moment during the postgame press conference at Pauley Pavillon. Well-respected Los Angeles sports columnist Bill Plaschke asked LeBron how the team was able to get schoolwork done while traveling all over the country. LeBron was about to answer the question, but Coach Joyce stepped in and was irritated that Plaschke questioned whether or not LeBron and the players were fulfilling academic requirements.

The same edition of the *L.A. Times* reporting on the schoolwork flap also included a story suggesting that LeBron's entourage members had their own entourage. That wasn't true at all. LeBron's "entourage" was his teammates. That's who he hung out with. And LeBron's mom, Gloria, didn't let anyone inside the "inner circle" if they weren't there before LeBron's popularity escalated.

For the most part, LeBron was level-headed and handled his fame admirably. Think about how any high school senior would act if he or she became a millionaire before graduation. Yes, at times LeBron was immature and arrogant, but a lot of high school star athletes can get full of themselves, even when they are not millionaires.

Most of the time during his high school career, LeBron was humble, loyal, charismatic, and a jokester, always wanting to have a good time and laugh with his

Jaleel White

friends. Usually it was just 'Bron being 'Bron. And the truth is, even as an NBA MVP and superstar, he's still the same way. ■

Author's Note

'm very proud to call Kris Belman a good friend. He and I met while we were working on our own projects. For me, it was working on the book *LeBron James: The Rise of a Star*, and for Kris, it was working on his senior project, which eventually turned into the film *More Than a Game*.

I'm also very proud that Kris asked me to be one of just three journalists extensively interviewed in the film. The others were Grant Wahl, who wrote the *Sports Illustrated* cover story on LeBron that ran in February 2002, and my former *Akron Beacon Journal* colleague Brian Windhorst. Kris even asked me to do some voice-overs for a few scenes while he was in Arizona working on the film.

Kris and I were blessed to have almost complete access to LeBron and the St. Vincent-St. Mary basketball team during LeBron's senior year. When most media members were kept outside during practices, Kris and I were inside watching those intense, college-like practices that coach Dru Joyce put his team through.

On many occasions, after Kris would get the footage he needed for that particular day and after I would get my interviews for the particular story that I was doing for my daily newspaper, the *Akron Beacon Journal*, the next day, Kris and I would go to a local pub, have a few beers, and just talk. We talked about how passionate we were about our projects. We talked about how lucky we were to be doing what we were doing and having the opportu-

nity to chronicle and follow someone as special as LeBron and his teammates.

We were sitting at the local pub after a St. Vincent-St. Mary practice, and we were talking about our careers and what we hoped to accomplish. I told Kris I wanted to write more books, which I have done. Kris said he wanted to be a filmmaker, which he's done.

At the same time, Kris and I never thought about trying to take advantage of LeBron's popularity for our own personal gain. We felt a sense of responsibility to tell stories about LeBron and his team from our unique perspectives—through his intimate images and through my rich and passionate descriptions.

While Kris was working on his project, he would occasionally call me and ask if I would like to see some of his progress. I would enthusiastically say, "Heck yeah." So we would arrange a homemade spaghetti dinner on Sundays. My beautiful and lovely wife, Tricia, who has a heart of gold, is Italian and is an absolutely great cook. She learned everything from her mother, Marietta.

Tricia would get up very early Sunday morning and make homemade pasta. It's a lot of work, but once she's done, and it's on the table, and she pours her homemade sauce over the noodles, it's pure heaven.

I'll never forget the Sunday Kris came to dinner to show his final project to me, Tricia, and a

few friends. It was another spaghetti Sunday. After dinner, Kris nervously gave us an introduction. He kept saying over and over, "I hope you like it. I hope you like it." I said, "Kris, relax. I'm sure you did a great job."

He put the DVD in, and we watched. We were blown away. We couldn't believe what we were seeing: footage revealing intimate access to the hottest high school basketball player and team in the world at the time—and no one had any of this exclusive footage except Kris.

After the 12-minute movie was done, and after the goose bumps on my arms receded, everyone was amazed at how personal and intimate the film was and how Kris featured the entire team and their close bond. It wasn't just a film about LeBron.

But after showing us the film, Kris then explained to us the biggest hurdle of all. He needed every player on the team to sign a release so that he would be able to use the film. If just one person decided they didn't want to sign the

release, Kris' project was useless.

I have to admit, I was somewhat concerned because at this time (it was the spring of LeBron's senior year, and he had already signed with an agent, Aaron Goodwin) LeBron already signed his contract with Nike for $90 million and declared, during a packed press conference at St. Vincent–St. Mary's gymnasium televised live on ESPN2, that he was forgoing his college eligibility and was headed straight to the NBA draft.

My thinking was that LeBron's agent, Aaron Goodwin, as well as LeBron's mother Gloria and others close to him, gave him explicit instructions not to sign anything—*anything*—without his agent and/or attorney (Cleveland lawyer Fred Nance) present.

Kris had arranged to show the film to LeBron and the team at the school during their lunch period. They all went into Patty Burdon's office. She was St. Vincent–St. Mary's public relations guru throughout LeBron's four years at the school. She'd had several children graduate from the school, and Patty and her husband, defense attorney Jim Burdon, were extensively involved in the school.

As the players started filing into Patty's office with their lunches, I was so nervous for Kris. I just *knew* LeBron wouldn't sign a release, because in essence, it would gave Kris the right to use his image and likeness in any type of film adaptation, which would mean a lot of money to be earned.

When everyone was in the office, Kris thanked all the guys for being gracious enough to allow him to spend several months with them. Then he showed the film. While the film played, the players watched intently, laughed at times, and fell quiet at others. When the film was over, they all were in amazement, like me and Tricia and my friends were when we had seen the film the day before at my home.

There were just a few minutes left before the bell would ring for the change of classes, so Kris said, "Hey guys, there's just one thing I need."

That's when my heart started racing, I felt a lump in my throat, and my stomach tied up in knots. I knew Kris absolutely needed the releases signed or he was done, and the project and all of the thousands of hours he put into it would go down the drain.

"Guys, in order for me to get a grade on this, I need you guys to sign a release saying you allow me to use you in the film."

Kris started passing around the release forms.

When LeBron got his release, he stood up and shouted, "My agent said I'm not supposed to sign anything."

I thought my worst fears became true, and I felt so bad for Kris.

Then, I couldn't believe my eyes. Just as fast as LeBron said those words, he grabbed a pen, signed his name, then raced out of the office so he could join all of his other buddies, who were frolicking around in the hallway for the last few minutes they had before the final bell rang. It was like he didn't want to miss any fun his friends were having in the hall.

I was so happy for Kris, and he breathed a big sigh of relief.

But as I look back on it, I realize exactly what happened. LeBron had always been a person who was loyal to his friends and to people whom he trusted. LeBron and his teammates had spent so much time with Kris that they trusted him and took him in as a friend.

LeBron knew exactly what he was doing when he signed that release, and he knew the ramifications. But what he did when he signed that release was to reward a friend for being a loyal, good-hearted, caring man.

That's why, for me personally, *More Than a Game* is more than a movie, because I saw where it started and how it ended, long before it hit the silver screen. And I'm extremely proud of what Kris produced and the fact that he let me be a part of it right from the start. ∎

Director Kris Belman poses with Dru Joyce II and Mike Brown before an advance screening of *More Than a Game*. Without LeBron's signature on a release six years before, Belman may have never had the chance to pursue filmmaking as a career, let alone release the full-length documentary.

LeBron is worldwide, as his arrival in front of his own image at an event in China can attest to. He's done it all, winning a gold medal and an MVP while remaining true to his Ohio roots. All that's left is an NBA title...

TRIUMPH
B O O K S